THE ~~COLLEGE~~ OF ART & DESIGN
UNIVERSITY COLLEGE

Farnham Campus, Falkner Road, Farnham, Surrey GU9 7DS
Return on or before the last date stamped below fines will be charged on overdue books

TABLE OF CONTENTS

PREFACE

JAPAN is a dynamic land of youth plunging into new ways, but it is also a land of old landscapes, structures, and customs as they were experienced by generations of poets. The intention of this book is to indicate something of Japanese poets of the 20th century. The sources of pleasure and truth are not restricted to the environment in which one was raised. One sophisticated to even a small degree learns this and yearns for what is out of reach. A poem in a strange language can be enticing. Curiosity, imagination, and discovery are parts of the process of understanding such a poem. Even a poor translator can be happy struggling to break through to a poet's form, intention, and inspiration, past the curtains of language. The poems offered here show work done both in the old forms and in new ways, as the poets sought fresher means to express what seems impossible to express. The blending of old and new, both always there in whatever style of writing is chosen, of that which is Japanese and that which is beyond a local environment, seems expressive of Bashō's words, "I do not seek to follow in the footsteps of the men of old, I seek the things they sought."

Poets' names have been shown in the Western way,

although it is the Japanese custom to write the family name before the personal name.

The translators gratefully thank the poets represented in this book for permission to use their work. Often the poets have been kindly helpful with corrections and suggestions for improving the translations. In all cases they or their heirs have approved the versions of what will be read here, but as English is not their own language they cannot be considered responsible for errors which we the translators might have made. When the inevitable errors are found, we hope they and our readers will be forgiving.

The poems by Shigenobu Takayanagi, Kiyoko Tsuda, and the first eight of those by Fumi Saitō were translated some years ago with the assistance of Prof. Makoto Ueda, and we express our gratitude to him for their inclusion in this book.

Our special thanks is given to Mr. Shirō Murano for two quotations from his prose writings. Prof. Hisao Kanaseki has also given permission for us to quote from prose he has written, and we wish to thank him too.

We acknowledge that some of these translations have previously appeared in the following journals: *Colorado State Review, East-West Review, The Literary Review, Literature East & West, Mundus Artium, Northwest Review, Puget Soundings, The Southern Review,* and *Transpacific.*

There are others we thank too, for both their help and their encouragement.

THE TRANSLATORS

INTRODUCTION

Contemporary Japanese poetry had its beginnings in the last twenty years of the 19th century. During that time Japan was under the first impact of modern contacts with the West. After centuries of isolation in a feudal culture with its own highly developed arts and social structures, the non-Oriental world of machines, military power, sciences, and democratic thought was open to intelligent and curious Japanese who were eager to learn and use the new. Under the Meiji regime Western ways were carefully observed, whether in theoretical fields or in practical matters. Among the books translated into Japanese at this time were several collections containing European and American poetry. From these began a romantic style of Japanese poetry-writing which developed into tendencies comparable to what was taking place in Europe and America at the same time. And these new styles of poetry were as strongly reactionary against the stagnations of conventional poetry as were the new movements in the West against the weaknesses of their literary traditions.

The *tanka* or *waka* form of Japanese poetry (five lines of five, seven, five, seven, and seven syllables, making a thirty-one-syllable poem) had been used at least since literature was first recorded in the classic mythology of the *Kojiki* in 712. It was the form of poetry in which all courtiers and socially acceptable persons were presumed to be able to compose throughout the culturally refined periods of Nara and Heian. Folk stories, the literary diaries, and the great novels were filled with tanka written by their characters, and tanka were frequently the base around which an incident was told. No aristocratic love affair could possibly be conducted without frequent formalized exchanges of tanka.

The 8th-century imperial collection of the *Manyōshū* has been called one of the world's greatest anthologies of poetry. Of the about forty-five hundred poems it contains, most are in tanka form, but a number are *chōka* or *nagauta* poems of greatly extended flexible length, also almost invariably in alternating five- and seven-syllable lines and refrains. After this anthology the *chōka* rarely reappeared. There were periods of writing Chinese-style poems, principally in the 9th and 19th centuries. Much Buddhist poetry was written in Chinese forms. (Some of this Chinese poetry has been translated by Burton Watson.) The tanka remained dominant until the 17th century and is still popular.

At its greatest in the early 15th century, the sublime poetry of the Nō drama varied in form, but moments of most-heightened emotions were in five- and seven-syllable lines, preceded by less regular lines, prose-poetry, and brief prose passages. As was tanka, it was written in the upper-class court language in a highly ornate and stately style, and made use of the usual Japanese poetic devices of serious puns, pivot words, and elaborate metaphors. Literary and geographic references, quotations, elaborations on an incident in the life of a known person, Buddhist beliefs and emotions, and the whole tradition of the previous centuries of Japanese culture were in the poetry of the Nō. And these influences more or less remained in Japanese poetry, at least into the 19th century.

A more popular type of verse, the *renga* or linked verse, also developed during these years. It joined three- and two-line halves of tanka together as a stanza series for any length, usually composed alternately by two or more poets. From these *renga* evolved the shorter seventeen-syllable, three-line *haiku* (*hokku, haikai*). The Tokugawa period, beginning in the 17th century, was an age of the rising of the merchant class and the lessening of the power of the aristocrats, under a military feudal government. Literacy became general. Arts were popularized, as in the puppet-Bunraku and Kabuki theaters, block prints, humorous and zesty or moralistic novels, and the writing of haiku by all classes of the population. Even great poets of the time, such as the sensitive and philosophic Bashō, remained within the limitations of the haiku form. The humorous verse *senryū* was also in the same form as haiku.

At the time of Japan's opening to foreigners in the mid-19th century very little was known of the outside world, but many Japanese had been eager to learn about the West for some time and only political pressures had restrained this desire. Nineteenth-century Japanese poets were composing in the tanka and haiku forms, usually in a stilted archaic speech considered proper to poetry—as was also common in the West at the same time. Clichés were admired, as well as re-using a line or the entire idea of another poet. The limited devices and conventional image associations had been worn threadbare. After more than a thousand years of tradition, the five- and seven-syllable lines had been forced into limitations that were of idea as well as of structure. Only certain viewpoints, approaches, and attitudes were properly allowed expression. The great, such as Bashō and Issa, managed to transcend such limitations and make of them the implements of a high art. But the great were not common.

Into this situation in 1882 the first translation of Western poetry was introduced, *Shintai Shishū* (A Collection of New Style Poems), translations of such poets as Gray, Longfellow, Bloomfield, Campbell, and Tennyson. It was a revelation to Japanese poets and began a romantic movement of imitation.

In 1889 *Omokage* (Semblances) appeared with translations of Goethe, Heine, Hoffman, Byron, and Shakespeare, done by Ōgai Mori and others. It was much better than the previous anthology.

In 1897 Tōson Shimazaki (1872–1943) published *Wakana-shū* (Seedlings), a book of his own Western-influenced poetry. His language remained pseudoclassic and his meter continued to alternate five and seven syllables on the old subjects of nature, love, and melancholy. But there was a newness, a sudden awareness of poetry's potentialities.

Other romantic poets appeared and soon many were reading Byron, Shelley, Keats, and Rossetti in English. Such articles began to appear by Japanese writers as "On Walt Whitman, Who Represents the Principle of Equality in the Literary World."

However, in 1905 *Kaichōon* (The Sound of the Tide) was printed, fifty-seven poems by twenty-nine poets—Italian, German, English, and the French Parnassians and Symbolists. In this volume the translator had daringly modified the Japanese literary language. The labels "Romantic Parnassian" and "Romantic Symbolist" were given to those inspired by this volume.

As romanticism and symbolism evolved into new formulations during the last years of the 19th century and the first of the 20th century, some of the poets of importance were the tanka poet Akiko Yosano (1878–1942), Suimei Kawai (1874–1965), a spoken-language poet who edited poetry magazines and encouraged young poets, Ariake Kambara (1876–1952), Hakushū Kitahara (1885–1942), and Rofū Miki (1889–1965).

But a very effective revolution in poetry soon broke out, establishing free verse in contemporary language. In *Gendai Shishū* (A Collection of Modern Japanese Poetry), Chikuma Shobō, Tokyo, 1958, Shirō Murano writes of this:

> The revolution to colloquial free verse was not merely rebellion or resistance against the old forms. Upheaval in poesy asked for a new order of poetry. The essential significance of this movement lies there.

About the reason for this revolution, several things
have been said by writers. Some say it was an indica-
tion of the political movement for democracy. Others
say that it was a manifestation of naturalism which was
started around that time in Japan. These elements
probably had some relationship to the revolution in
poetry. But the more essential and direct reason was
the new discovery of poetic estheticism or reality
which was adapted to the times.

. . . In order to express this new poetic reality,
visual elements by image replaced the musical elements
that had been in the previous poetry.

There were new magazines and further experiments in
the use of a more natural language. Around 1908 there was
a colloquial free-verse movement reflecting the influences
of Whitman, Baudelaire, and Rimbaud. Also, a group of
people's poets flourished, and there was a school of
humanism.

At first the interest in Whitman had been in his being a
democratic, humanistic, non-traditional "international."
Translations of his poetry and books about him helped in-
troduce democratic thought into Japanese poetry and the
use of the colloquial language was furthered. After 1918
he was more neglected in Japan but still much admired.

Between 1912 and 1922 free verse matured. The princi-
pal figures in this development were Kōtarō Takamura
(1883–1956) and Sakutarō Hagiwara (1886–1942). That is
why this anthology begins with them. They were born in the

same decade as Pound, Cocteau, James Joyce, D. H. Lawrence, Wallace Stevens, William Carlos Williams, and many others who are considered to be the beginners of what we call the modern. The tanka and haiku given in translations here were also written in this century when a consciousness of what was "modern" in literature was universal.

After several poets had tried to establish the possibility of colloquial free verse, in 1914 Kōtarō Takamura published *Dōtei* (Itinerary). This was the first real proof that colloquial free verse could stand as poetry. A sculptor and the son of a famous sculptor, he had spent four years in France, England, and America before returning to Japan in 1910. Seven of his poems are presented here.

It is Sakutarō Hagiwara who is acknowledged to be the greatest of modern Japanese poets. He is one of those most widely influencing younger poets, and no other poet of modern Japan has been more frequently translated than he. From his spiritual solitude, influenced by Poe, Dostoevski, Schopenhauer, and Nietzsche, he developed a unique symbolic music of his own which in his later years ended in ennui and nihilism. He was one of the most successful poets in the new idiom, using the current language in place of the formal archaic diction of classical literature. *Tsuki ni Hoeru* (Howling at the Moon) was published in 1917 and *Ao-neko* (Blue Cat) in 1923, and he published further poetry as well as essays and criticism. The best of his work belongs with the great literature of the world. In his poetry the long tradition of Japanese sensitivity and esthetic skill, as well as the essence of philosophic Buddhism, is revealed in a new and intense way which is not entirely lost in translations. Five of his poems are included in this anthology.

The surrealist movement developed in Japan after 1925. In that year another important book of translations appeared, *Gekka no Ichigun* (A Group in the Moonlight). It contained the work of seventy recent French poets, including Cocteau, Apollinaire, Jammes, and Jacob.

Probably the most noted Japanese surrealist poet is Junzaburō Nishiwaki (b. 1896). He studied English at Oxford and his first book of poems was published in London in 1925, *Spectrum*, written in English. He called himself a surnaturalist, was Western in outlook, became a professor of English literature, and has published essays and translations as well as poetry. His translations of Eliot's *The Waste Land* and his own poetry made him one of the most influential of moderns. He is not included in this anthology because he himself often writes in English or translates his own poems, and much of his work can be found elsewhere.

Others influenced by contemporary French poets have been divided into a modern school and a lyric school. Under the former heading are included Yukio Haruyama (b. 1902), Katsue Kitasono (b. 1902), Iku Takenaka (b. 1904; four of his poems are in this volume), Etsurō Sakamoto (b. 1906), Ichirō Andō (b. 1907), and Shirō Murano (b. 1901). Murano will be mentioned again later. The lyricists include Tatsuji Miyoshi (1900–1964, seven poems here), Fuyuji Tanaka (b. 1895), Shizuo Itō (1906–53, two poems here), and Michizō Tachihara (1914–39). Many of these poets have

continued writing to the present. Most of the poets translated here will be found mentioned in *Japanese Literature of
the Shōwa Period: A Guide to Japanese Reference and Research
Materials*, by Joseph K. Yamagiwa.

In *The Poetry of Living Japan* by Takamichi Ninomiya and
D. J. Enright, and in *An Anthology of Modern Japanese Poetry*
by Rikutarō Fukuda and Ichirō Kōno, brief biographies and
translated poems are given for most of these poets as well
as for many others, including some of the most experimental. Donald Keene too has written of these moderns in
the introduction to his *Modern Japanese Literature*. Much
additional material will be found in the magazine *Poetry*'s
special *Contemporary Poetry in Japan* number, May 1956,
edited and translated by Satoru Satō and Constance Urdang,
as well as in the *Modern Japanese Literature* number of *The
Literary Review*, autumn 1962, edited and translated by
Makoto Ueda.

Among the many poetry magazines in Japan was *Shi to
Shiron* (Poetry and Poetics), 1928 to 1931, fourteen quarterly volumes of over two hundred pages each, in which was
printed the latest work of such poets as Valéry, Cocteau,
Aragon, Breton, Eluard, Joyce, Pound, Lawrence, Cum-
mings, Stein, and Eliot.

After 1925 a proletarian school developed briefly. Among
its poets were Shigeharu Nakano (b. 1902) and Shigeji
Tsuboi (b. 1898). Tsuboi was a member of the Japan Proletarian Writers' League before the war, and he was among
those founding the New Japan Literature Society afterward.
Seven of his poems are in this book, and he has been fre-

quently translated by others also. Most of the proletarian poets either stopped writing poetry or turned to other styles and affiliations after the rise of Japanese nationalism.

Independent poets were writing too. One of these was Mitsuharu Kaneko (b. 1895). He was first a symbolist, then a realist, then a nihilist. In Europe for a number of years, he was influenced by Rimbaud, Baudelaire, Verhaeren, and Whitman, and he also spent time in China. Most of his postwar poems are an indirect social commentary. Five of his poems are here, including several in protest of Japan's last war.

Shirō Murano (b. 1901) published his first book of poetry in 1926. Earlier he had written haiku. Today he is one of the leading poets as well as an important intellectual and critic. Along with Yoshiaki Sasazawa (b. 1898, two poems here), he introduced the *Neue Sachlichkeit* movement from Germany into Japan. Especially admired by the younger generation, he is a positive link between Sakutarō Hagiwara and the new generation of poets. His 1939 poems on gymnastics are especially noted for originality and modernity. His recent work has a strongly philosophical tone from his thoughts on Buddhism. Perhaps something of the variety of range in his poetic voice can be glimpsed through the ten translations given here.

Shimpei Kusano (b. 1903) was first an anarchist, then a romantic mystic and devotee of estheticism. He spent eighteen years in China. A leader of those who were against the intellectual in poetry, he is still very active in modern poetry groups. Although he is considered one of the major poets, his work is not represented here as it seems to require a special technique of translation to convey his style.

After Japan's defeat the postwar poets whose mental themes were based on the poetics of Eliot called themselves Poets of the Waste Land. Among them were Ryūichi Tamura (b. 1923, one poem here), Saburō Kuroda (b. 1919, three poems here), Masao Nakagiri (b. 1919, one poem here), and Nobuo Ayukawa (b. 1920, three poems here).

Following the high note of this movement, other varying attitudes developed, expressed by such poets as Minoru Yoshioka (b. 1919, three poems here), and Shuntarō Tanikawa (b. 1931, five poems here). Today's poetry, like that of other countries, has many aspects. The poets seem unafraid to be themselves and individualistic, and each seems to be searching for himself, sometimes hopefully.

Murano closes his brief history of modern Japanese poetry in *Gendai Shishū* by saying:

> Thus Japanese poetry which . . . since 1882 has been experiencing various changes in literary attitudes has close interaction today with poets and poetries of various countries of the world. It has come to have an internationality and a poetic range of themes and subjects common with all.
>
> But the mentality and form of modern poetry is a precious heritage from previous poets since Meiji times. And it is with the tradition of the Japanese

language, long polished by predecessors, that poets today are proceeding toward the later half of this century.

At present there are innumerable poetry magazines being published in Japan, and considerable activity among the poets centered in Tokyo. Too, such organizations as the Japan P.E.N. Club and the Modern Poets Association keep poets in communication with one another.

Contemporary Western poets are now often quickly translated into Japanese or read in their original language. Noted translators such as Rikutarō Fukuda have made anthologies of their own translations of the most recent Western poetry, often after actually meeting and talking with the American and European poets. University students who study a foreign language or literature learn to read and discuss a foreign poetry in their classrooms as well as to write a thesis on some European or American poet. Western poetry is no longer an oddity in Japan, nor it is now accepted uncritically. Matured readers may reject it and prefer what is being written in their own country. Many poets are students of the old Chinese poetry as well as of their own classical poetry of the past, and criticism has a sophisticated basis.

It would be wrong to overemphasize Western influences in what is being written today. What was once foreign has become assimilated and is now largely Japanese. The best poets still remain more shaped by their Japanese environment and traditions than by what comes newly from other places. Like poets everywhere, they respond to what is actual in their lives and in a way true to their own personal development within their own culture. For instance, the word *sabishii* ("lonely," "solitary") remains frequent, as it was in the old poetry. The modern Japanese is as sharply aware of this concept as the poets of Japan's past; he lives with it. Nor is nihilism new to Japanese, and it is usual for it to be seen through a Buddhist perspective. The tanka personal emotion, the haiku moment of simply seeing, and even the *senryū* humor are often found extended or in separate lines of the free-verse poems. Being suggestive rather than fully expressive often remains as a quality of new work. This is as it should be and inescapable for the sincere poet. Japan has had more than a thousand years of highly developed arts and crafts, of aristocracy and elegance coexisting with simplicity, asceticism, and the natural, with robust folk activities, or the cities' slum dwellers and newly rich merchants. And there were centuries of political and economic struggles that brought all face to face with the most pessimistic precepts of Buddhism. Viewpoints resulting from these are still in the literature as they are in its writers, and what seems Western is often little more than an outward shape combined with that which is common to all creative men in all places and ages.

Poetic forms change through time and by local evolvements, but the matter of being a poet is something beyond a current fashion in technique or style of expression.

This anthology includes a number of tanka and haiku. Today in Japan there are still more who write in these old forms than who are using free verse. Actually, it has been estimated, some million attend group meetings under a master and continue for years to work at improving their skill at composing these little poems. Office workers, factory workers, housewives, students, all can join others of their associates in these endeavors. Groups are sponsored by newspapers for a fee, and large companies provide their employees with a tanka or haiku master to give instruction, advice, and criticism as part of the regular recreation programs. Many groups have their own little magazines, and newspapers and popular magazines carry tanka and haiku columns. Usually an individual chooses just one of these forms and concentrates his creative work within it.

The benefits and limitations of this mass poetry-producing can be easily imagined. For most of its participants it is a very good thing, but it cannot be expected to result in quantities of great poetry. Really good poets are rare in any environment. It does tend to cause a smug attitude toward other types of poetry so that the really individualistic creative poet is considered an oddity by many of these conventional writers. Making tanka or haiku under such circumstances can become both limited and limiting as far as real artistry is concerned. However, as a solitary exercise in craftsmanship and reaction to experience it is often of value to the writer and gives pleasure to his friends who are the readers. At its best it is undeniably worthy of being called true poetry.

Concurrent with the development of free verse, some poets of the old forms modernized. New subject matter became allowable, new syllabic patterns, variations in the typography. Startling attitudes were admired by some schools of tanka and haiku, and the inclusion of modern words and objects. However, usually tanka are still written in an old-style classical language and this is generally true of haiku.

As there is now so much available in English on the subject of tanka and haiku, it will not be explained here in detail. The examples given in this book have been chosen as a few among countless. It is hoped they will reveal a little of some of the various kinds that are now being written. Some will not seem different from those written centuries ago, and others will present their modernity conspicuously.

Although tanka had been able to achieve excellence in the old classical anthologies, the 8th-century *Manyōshū*, the 10th-century *Kokinshū*, and the 13th-century *Shin-Kokinshū*, it had become monotonous and manneristic by the Tokugawa period of 1603 to 1867. After the Meiji Restoration in 1868 this weakness persisted; gradually, however, a consciousness of the new age came to be awakened among tanka writers too. In 1901 *Midaregami* (Tangled Hair) was published, a tanka collection by the woman poet Akiko Yosano (1878–1942). She has been often translated. *Myōjō* (Morning Star), the magazine of her group, influenced many other tanka poets. They expressed themselves with romanticism and estheticism, but gradually these became manneristic too, and a number of poets with a new viewpoint became recognized. They studied the *Manyōshū* and their work was based on realism.

Among these was Mokichi Saitō (1882–1953; thirteen of his tanka are in this anthology), whose first book of tanka was published in 1913. It was he who was largely responsible for the restoration of strength to this ancient form. From his magazine *Araragi* (Yew Tree) several other noted and capable poets developed, but at the same time there were a number of tanka poets who wrote in different styles. Even now the schools of tanka are many and varied.

It was around 1890 that haiku began to be written with a consciousness of their being a real art for moderns as they had been for poets of the past such as Bashō (1644–94), Buson (1714–81), and Issa (1763–1827). Shiki Masaoka (1867–1902) broke from previous mannerisms, stressing the importance of realism. This was continued by two other haiku poets, Kyoshi Takahama (1874–1959, eleven haiku here) and Hekigodō Kawahigashi (1873–1937, two haiku here). The attitude of Takahama was romantic and conservative, while that of Kawahigashi was strictly realistic as well as experimental. This experimenting was to free haiku from such limitations as its containing seventeen syllables and its season-word, and others further developed Kawahigashi's movement. The romantic school of Kyoshi Takahama produced many haiku poets, but later its conservatism led some to leave this group and form their own groups, some of which tried to make a freer haiku.

The haiku of Shigenobu Takayanagi (b. 1923, six haiku here) are examples of breaking away from conventions of the form, though they still remain within a quite constricted framework. In spite of their new variations in syllable numbers, lines, and subjects, they remain unmistakably haiku, but with a new feeling of distortion of the expected.

Many other tanka and haiku might have been presented in place of or in addition to those chosen, but those offered here were felt to be representative of what is currently being done in these fields and will provide a comparison with the longer poems.

ON TRANSLATION

This book is not the first anthology of contemporary Japanese poetry in English and there are now various sources of translated Japanese poems, some of which are named in the list given at the end of this book. Literary journals have sometimes included such translations, occasionally as a group or in a special issue. Articles on Japanese poets and poetry are not rare, especially in those journals devoted to Asian materials, such as *The Japan Quarterly*, *The East-West Review*, *Literature East & West*, *The Journal of Asian Studies*, *Journal of the American Oriental Society,* and the *Kokusai Bunka Shinkōkai* (KBS Bulletin). They also frequently contain translations.

As so much material already exists, and the poetry has been several times presented in historical order, the editors here have felt free to choose what they particularly found significant and amenable to translation. The more experimental and avant-garde has been omitted as of interest mostly to those who have already been made aware of it elsewhere. The chosen pieces are some of the many it was believed could be translated justly and read with a comprehension of the poet and his intentions. In most cases they have not been previously translated. They are intended as an extension of what has already been done in this field and not, in themselves, as a complete presentation of modern Japanese poetry Nor can they fully represent the work of any one poet. But it is hoped they will arouse sympathetic understanding in poets writing in English, in general readers of Western poetry, and in those interested in knowing more of Asian materials. Perhaps in the future we can do an entire volume containing the work of just one of the poets included here.

The first group of Westerners to bring anything of Far Eastern literature to Europe were members of the Catholic missions. Jesuit missionaries were in China as early as the 13th century, and among those of later centuries were scholars and linguists who took back to France their translations of Chinese classics. Portuguese Jesuits came to Japan in the 16th century, and Dominicans and Franciscans followed in both China and Japan.

China and Japan were both opened to the West in the mid-19th century, and as early as 1865 James Legge was publishing translations from Chinese literature. Lafcadio Hearn came to Japan in 1890 and soon began writing books which revealed something of the country's culture. A book on Chinese literature was done by H. A. Giles in 1901, and in 1902 Captain F. Brinkley's *China, Its History, Arts and Literature* was published in four volumes. W. G. Aston was writing on Japanese literature just before the end of the 19th century, and other early writers on Japan were Captain F. Brinkley, Ernest Fenollosa, and B. H. Chamberlain, who produced a book on Japanese poetry in 1911. Much interesting material can be found in the old issues of *Transactions of the Asiatic Society of Japan*.

Ezra Pound's early interest in Chinese ideographs and poetry, and in Japanese Nō drama and haiku, is well known and a large literature exists about it and its influences on Yeats and the Imagists.

However, it was not until Arthur Waley began publishing his series of books of translations from Chinese poetry in 1919 that anything of Far Eastern poetry was popularly known in English. Waley also translated a number of volumes of early Japanese literature, including tanka. He really might be said to be the one man who stimulated further translations in this field. Previous translations had not been very effective. Those making them had been primarily linguists and the efforts of mastering the Chinese or Japanese language did not leave much energy for the consideration of literary qualities. Usually the standard for poetry translations was earlier 19th-century English poetry of the popular type. Often a tanka or haiku was distorted into some form acceptable to one with a taste for the most conventional, such as a rhymed couplet, or a quatrain in iambics with a number of adjectives added. Rarely were the translators poets or even interested in poetry. But Arthur Waley showed that it was possible to make a translation which conveyed considerable of the original poem's style and content and was at the same time good reading and a stimulating discovery. Now we accept as commonplace the translations from Chinese and Japanese just as we would translations from European languages, and many are of a high standard of excellence, though, unfortunately, this still cannot be said of all of them.

Much has been written on the problems of translation. All acknowledge there can be no such thing as a perfect translation. But some translations appear to be better than others and are of much interest for what they reveal of a poet, his techniques, and his culture.

Today it is certainly as reasonable for a Westerner to want to know something of Japanese poetry as to have an interest in any European poetry. Without translation the poetry of ancient Greece and Rome and the Italian Renaissance, as well as that of present-day European countries, would be unavailable to most of us. As it is, much of Western culture is based on knowledge gained through such translations.

However, there are special problems in dealing with the Japanese language and poetic forms. They do not resemble material that has been in our previous experience. Also rhyme and meter-stress as used in the West are neither traditional nor practical in Japanese. Even Arthur Waley remarked that "of all poetries Japanese poetry is the most untranslatable."

Hisao Kanaseki writes about one aspect of this in his article "Haiku and Modern American Poetry," in *The East-West Review*, winter 1967–68:

> In our writing we use, needless to say, a great many Chinese ideograms or *kanji*, poetry being no exception. Then, these ideograms, or characters, are essentially symbols and often pictorial symbols, and therefore they have visual values. We Japanese often consider that certain combinations of strokes in *kanji* are more beautiful visually than others. . . . All those words which have been used by Japanese traditional poets have indeed such visual beauty that it is usually quite impossible to appreciate it unless you see the characters written or printed on the paper. . . . From ancient times till fairly recently all poems in Japan were written with brush on a sheet of paper by the poet's own hand, and no matter how excellent one might actually be as a poet, if one's calligraphy were clumsy or inelegant, it would have been the common verdict that he was a bad poet.

An approach to translation can be a matter of literary taste, whether one prefers the strictly formal or a more free style. Also it depends on whether one believes a translator functions primarily to convey to a reader as nearly as he can a sense of what the poem was like as the poet made it, or to create a new poem in English suggested by the original one.

As Japanese poetry is almost the only poetry in the entire world which did not in the past make use of rhyme and meter as we know them, surely this uniqueness is in itself worth preserving when tanka and haiku are made available in English. Now, when arts are internationally appreciated, and the very differences in craftsmanship and expression of thought are intriguing, it would seem the function of an interpreter to preserve these fundamental differences, to show how a culture's poets have evolved a different pattern for expression, and that previously unknown solutions to problems of artistic creativity can be perceptively stimulating as well as of great interest technically. This should still be so even if the differences are due mainly to differences in the language structure.

Readers of English today, if they have any interest at all in such matters as poetry or Oriental art forms, can be presumed to have the knowledgeability to grasp the intent of a particular grouping of words. Respect for such readers, as well as for the individual poet, would seem to make it desirable to attempt to present the poem as it was first written, as much as possible. The Japanese old forms are of such brevity it can be assumed that the best poets knew what they were doing and did it intentionally. If one word, one image, preceded another, it was because that was the way the poet wanted it to be. If the piece was fragmentary, that too was intentional. Any sparsity of adjectives was purposeful. He knew his own language and how to use it. The English language and the viewpoints of its readers need not be considered too limited for such simplicity.

Working at translating is a fascinating puzzle that is un-solvable. That is one reason why so many cannot resist a try. Working on this volume reaffirmed that there is no perfect solution to the problems of translation. However, it was done as an attempt to show the poems as they were, as nearly as we were able to, rather than an attempt to improve upon the originals. In most cases it was possible to retain the original line order and order of images. Sometimes we kept a Japanese verb form even when it might seem another would be preferred, though a purist could argue that the two languages are so different that such details are irrele-vant. Since for each word used others could have been substituted, the results are unavoidably colored by the imaginations and limitations of the translators and are debat-able. But a word was not omitted even in cases where the poem might have seemed better without it. For instance, the frequent modifying of the word "night" by some such word as "solitary" or "melancholy" was retained though it probably would not be written in that way by a modern Western writer. Such modification could be accounted for as one thing retained from the classic tanka which goes back to the 8th century, and even a modern Japanese poet has become so used to such a concept of "night" that he uses it in a natural way, just as a Western poet still retains habits from the literature of the past. Of course many modern Japanese poets consciously strive to avoid such traditional word patterns, but such a difference between poets is some-thing that a translator should attempt to show in his work. As Japanese sentence structure is in inverse order to that of

English, to keep the order of images it was sometimes necessary to have inverted sentences. In many cases this seemed preferable, and the results more interesting than if a more conventional English pattern were followed. Also, an attempt was made to preserve the original tone of language, something which is really impossible to do, but perhaps a slight echo of the original remains in some of these translations. For some poems footnotes have been added.

To work with these poems was fascinating and enjoyable. We wish to conclude by expressing to the poets who made it possible our sincere respect and gratitude. This volume's purpose will have been fulfilled if a reader can find himself becoming suddenly aware of the particular voices of any few poets among those presented here.

Part One

FREE VERSE

KŌTARŌ TAKAMURA
(1883–1956)

高村光太郎

A Man Sharpening a Knife

In silence a knife is being sharpened.
Though the sun is already sinking, it is still being sharpened.
The back and the front tightly placed,
the whetting water changed, it is being sharpened again.
What on earth is intended to be made?
As though without knowing even that,
concentrating the mood of the moment in his brow,
behind green leaves, the man sharpens the knife.
Bit by bit this man's sleeve tears.
The mustache of this man becomes white.
Resentment? Necessity? A vacant mind?
This man is simply endless.
Is he pursuing the nth degree?

Mars Is Out

Mars is out.

After all, what should be done? The query
brings back to a beginning a way of thought it was hard for
  me to follow.
After all, doesn't it matter?
No, no, infinitely no.
It is best to wait, and with the first strength
it is best to destroy your weakness that is quick with such
  a question.
To think of a predicted result is not decent.
To live with the right source,
only that is pure.
In order to stir up your being further,
once again raise up your head high.
Shining right over this dark Komagome Hill that is asleep
  and silent,
it is good to see that really red star.

Mars is out.

A cold blast makes a rattle-rattle sound in the honey locust
  pods.
A rutting dog dashes around madly.
If I step on fallen leaves
and pass the bushes,
a cliff.

Mars is out.

I do not know
what a human being must do.
I do not know
what a human being should try to get.
I think
that a human being can become part of nature.
I am feeling
that a human being is great because he is equal to
    nothingness.
Oh I am shaken,
how hopeful to be equal to nothingness!
Even nothingness is destroyed
by natural spreading.

Mars is out.

The sky turns around behind it.
Innumerable far worlds are coming up.
Unlike poets of old days, I do not
see a twinkling of angels in it anymore.
I just listen
to what is like profound waves of ether.
And simply
the world is wonderful.
Its weird grace filled with things unknown
presses toward me tightly, tightly.

Mars is out.

Plum Wine

The bottle of plum wine made and left by dead Chieko,
dully stagnant with ten years' weight, holds the light,
and in the amber of a wine cup congeals like a jewel-ball.
When alone late at night in the cold time of early spring
please have this, she said.
I think of the one who left this after dying.
Being threatened with the anxiety of a broken mind,
with the distressing idea of ruin before long,
Chieko took care of things around her.
Seven years of madness finished with death.
The fragrant sweetness of this plum wine found in
    the kitchen
quietly, quietly, I appreciate.
Even the roar of the world of frenzied angry waves
can hardly violate this moment.
When one wretched life is looked straight at
the world just distantly surrounds it.
Now the night wind has stopped.

Another Rotating Thing

Half wet with spring rain, the morning newspaper,
a little heavy in my hands,
is cutting into shreds the letters and characters of this life.
Iron and gunpowder of the world and the titans behind them
are turning once again in a direction which is difficult to
    stop.
With a little oil smudge, printing type tells it.

The revolving of the solid earth cannot be ended.
I flick off cherry blossom petals that were brought in stuck
    to the newspaper.
Inside myself another solid earth rotates.

The Itinerary

In front of me no road
behind me a road is made
ah the natural
a father
an immense father that caused me to stand by myself
do protect me and do not take your eyes from me
continually fill me with a vigor of the father
for the sake of this far journey
for the sake of this far journey.

Winter Has Come

Definitely winter has come.
The evergreen shrub's white flowers have disappeared.
The ginko trees have turned into brooms.

Like a sharp sharp piercing, winter has come.
Everyone dislikes winter.
Deserted by grasses and trees, run away from by insects,
    winter has come.

Winter,
come to me, come to me.
I have winter's strength, winter is my victim.

Permeate through, penetrate into!
Make fires break out! Bury with snow!
Like a sharp knife, winter has come.

Difficult Chieko

Chieko sees what cannot be seen,
hears what cannot be heard.

Chieko goes to places one cannot go,
does what cannot be done.

Chieko does not see the me that really exists,
yearns for me in back of me.

Chieko throws away the heaviness of suffering now,
wanders out to a vast infinite sphere of esthetic
    consciousness.

Though hearing her voice calling me over and over,
Chieko does not have a ticket for the human world anymore.

SAKUTARŌ HAGIWARA

(1886–1942)

萩原朔太郎

The Swimmer

The swimmer's body stretches out slanting,
two arms reach out together lengthily,
the swimmer's heart is transparent like a jellyfish,
the swimmer's eyes are hearing the sound of
    suspended bells,
the swimmer's spirit watches the moon over the water.

Death of a Frog

A frog was killed.
A circle of children raised their hands.
All together
lovely
bloody hands they raised.
The moon rose.
On the hill a man is standing.
Under the hat is his face.

You Frogs

You frogs!
Inside the tangle of blue pampas grass and reeds
frogs seem to be bulging out whitely.
In the evening scene filled with rainfall
the *gyo, gyo, gyo, gyo* of crying frogs.

Striking and beating on the utterly dark ground,
this is a night violent with rain and wind.
On the chilled grasses and leaves too
frogs draw in a soft breath,
the *gyo, gyo, gyo, gyo* of crying frogs.

You frogs!
My being is not far away from you.
With a lamp in my hand I
was watching the surface of the dark garden,
was watching with fatigued mind leaves of grasses and trees
    sagging in rain.

Wanting To Be Walking Among Crowds

I always want the city,
want to be inside the lively crowds of the city.
Crowds are things like huge waves with emotions.
They are groups of vigorous wills and desires pouring into
    every place.
Oh in the plaintive twilight of spring,
to want the shade between building and building in the
    complicated city,
to go along tossed about inside the huge crowds, how
    joyful it is.
Look, this sight of crowds that go flowing by.
One wave overlapping upon another wave,
the waves making innumerable shadows, and the shadows
    move on swaying.
The distress and sorrows of each one of the people all
    disappear there among the shadows, leaving no trace.
Oh with how tranquil a mind I go walking along this
    street.
Oh this joyful shadow of the great love and innocence.
The sensation of being carried along beyond the joyful
    waves becomes almost like weeping.
In the desolate twilight of a day of spring,
these groups of lovers swimming under the eaves from
    building to building,
where and in what way do they go flowing along I wonder?
My sorrowful gloominess is covered up in the one big

shadow on the earth, flowing waves of the drifting innocence.

Oh I want to go on being tossed by these waves of crowds no matter where, no matter where.

Waves far ahead on the horizon look indistinct.

Toward one, only one direction, let me flow along.

Buddha
(The World's Mystery)

In hilly country where red soil is abundant,
inside a deserted cavern there is one man sleeping.
You are not shell, not bone either, not material either,
and in sandy places of dried-up beach weeds
not like an old watch corroded with rust either.
Ah, are you the shadow of "truth," or a ghost,
endlessly, endlessly, sitting in that place?
Mummified one! Living like a miraculous fish!
At the end of this unendurably desolate wild land
the sea roars to the sky,
the booming of huge tidal waves is heard coming in from far off.
Do you hear it with your ears,
eternal man, Buddha?

SAISEI MURŌ
(1889–1962)

室生犀星

After a Music Concert

The minds of people were rather fatigued with
   profundity,
making pleasant rippling waves
as though saturated.
People were speaking in low voices about subtle words
   that music gives.
After a stairway to a lawn,
stepping on the sprouting blades of the lawn,
already walking toward a park with street lights,
a person with a beautiful younger sister,
a person with a happy woman friend,
a person with a wife,
they all in a similar way of fatigue
were walking with a strangely vivid and lively
   excitement.
And I too, following along after that crowd,
aware of my own solitary footsteps,
was walking toward the park near springtime.

Trout Shadows

Trout with moles on their backs
are clearly swimming along the river shore in sunlight.
In several rows
their gentle bodies are shining.
On the white sand their shadows
like shadow pictures
are becoming bigger, becoming smaller,
and at times become dim.
Even the shadows of the water making beads
go falling to the sandy bottom.

When astonished by just a slight noise
the trout scatter like flowers
and gather again.
One trout, handsome, and larger than the others in the
group,
perhaps leading the group sometimes,
comes out a little upstream in the current,
or proudly swims up high to the surface
and turns over flipping.
Completely silent ripples are made.
After that there is only the smell of young leaves on the
    river bank.

A Camel

In thin shade
a camel that is fastened,
like an aged man,
mumbling and mumbling, is eating things all day long.
His tent is like a sky with snow,
hanging grey and dismal.
Without speaking the camel
keeps moving his mouth all day.

A Baby-Tending Song

When snow is falling a baby-tending song is heard.
It has been occurring for a long time.
From the window, from the door,
from the sky,
a baby-tending song is heard.
But I have never had the experience of hearing a baby-
    tending song.
For me who did not know a person called mother in
    childhood
the memory of such a song could not be imagined to exist.

But strangely
on a day when snow is falling it is heard,
a song I have not experienced hearing anywhere is heard.

City River

Rain is falling down quietly.
On the river it is hushed,
making a delicate sound.
Occasionally a streetcar passes reflecting shadows on the
    dull leaden surface.
Several groups of barges are tied up.

Though boats touched by the rain
seem to move
they are fastened.
From the eaves of a roof a streak of smoke rises up.
From a window a child eagerly watches a streetcar on the
    bridge for as long as it is there.

Figures of people on the street all reflect upon the
    water and
quietly they disappear.
The smoke still rises up.
A woman who looks like the mother of the child
washes a green bunch of leeks.
In the hushed rainfall everything has turned into a fantasy
    of the bridge.

Inside a Deep Isolation

When a musician steps down off the stage,
when he steps down, sent off with the clapping of a fine
   crowd of people,
what an intense and deserted isolation he must feel.
In spite of that thunder of admiration
how deeply a fine musician, outside the bounds of the
   crowd of people,
must love with a passion the height of isolation that is his.

An Unfinished Poem

Red red glow of evening,
under it tightly crowded streets and houses.
Looking at them I become fatigued.
What comes from there in a reflection?
What comes from there to pervade my being
is voices and voices of peddlers at twilight time,
mixed with the smell of the lonely rainfall of late autumn,
voices and voices of various lives.
Leaning against a window I am listening to it.

尾崎喜八

A Word

I have to select a word for material.
It should be talked about in the smallest possible
    amount and
have a deep suggestiveness like nature,
bloom from inside its own self,
and at the edge of the fate encircling me
it will have to become darkly and sweetly ripened.

Of a hundred experiences it always
has to be the sum total of only one.
One drop of water dew
becomes the harvest of all dewdrops,
a dark evening's one red point of light
is the night of the whole world.

And after that my poem
like a substance entirely fresh,
released far away from my memory,
the same as a scythe in a field in the morning,
the same as the ice on a lake in spring,
will suddenly begin to sing from its own recollection.

Winter Field

Now, over the field,
evening hangs suspended like a gigantic harp.

Frost binds the ridges solemnly severed furrow from
    furrow;
the long harp-sound of the wind runs by,
one first white star
strikes the highest note.

Winter fades widely, widely like an ancient;
though spring is yet far away
presentiments already hover between heaven and earth.

I step on this late earth that is growing dark
and throw seeds from my hand
overflowing like the evening sun
and heavy because of faith in seeds.

They sink
like stuff that serves deeply,
to transform the nights under the ground
and enlighten gradually the far daybreak.

A pure and clear condensation is felt.
Now, within the greyish silence around,
my being is a reverent anthem.

And already hearing
(the harvest field like a festival,
burning noon kingfisher colored)
June like the sea.

Being

Frequently I am impelled to stand still,
as though to authenticate the distance to an object.
That distance is being replenished,
behold, by thick whirlwinds and billions of air particles.

Yesterday I watched smoke of field fires ascend from several
    places of this plateau,
today listen to faint birds in a forest of fallen leaves.
For ten days I have not heard news of the city,
undulations of fields and mountains where clouds gather and
narrow pathways run through blue-green withered
    grasses and
occasional trains descend a ravine shouldering cliffs
    and . . .

Yes, existing clear and separate from each other,
being strong indeed in their final essence and fate,
aspects of objects always express their own most proper
    plendors.
In this way, being entirely alone,
to all phenomena of the world
I give praise for original corresponding splendors.

MITSUHARU KANEKO
(b. 1895)

金
子
光
晴

Song of a Jellyfish

Swaying, swaying,
tossing, tossing,
eventually I
could be seen through like this.

But to be swayed is not a comfortable thing, you know.

From the outside I can be seen through. Look!
Inside my digestive organs
is a toothbrush with worn-out bristles
and also a small amount of yellowish water.

That dirty-looking thing called my soul
does not exist anymore now.
Together with the tubes of my belly
it was snatched away by the waves.

Me? What I am
is a thing of emptiness, you know,

emptiness swayed by the wave
and again swayed back and forth by the waves.

Shriveling up and then soon afterward
opening wisteria-purple,
night after night
burning a lamp.

No, that which is being swayed about actually
is only the soul which has lost the body
that is the soul's wrapping
of thin rice paper.

No, no, so much emptiness came from
swaying, swaying,
tossing, tossing pain's
fatigued shadow which is all that it is!

Cuckoos

Deep in a forest where it rains
cuckoos cry.

Beyond pale darkness
their echoes respond.

Elegant-looking tips of the trees
are hearing the silent fog that is coming down,
that fog turning into drops of water on twigs
and softly dripping down.

On the path that continues into the fog
I stop walking and listen
to voices of lonely cuckoos.

Droplets of water make a separating curtain,
and from an eternal end is heard
that monotonous repetition.

I look back at the lengthy time
of my short life,
estrangements of affection and
a period of many betrayals.

Beloved persons who have departed too,
scattered-away friends too,
all of them have gone inside this fog
and perhaps exist somewhere in the end of the fog.

Now already there is no way to search.
From end to end

the enveloping fog thickens and thickens.
All the loneliness for what cannot be regained
is swept along very quickly.

Here and there in the ocean of fog
like spirit and spirit that call to each other
cuckoos are crying,
cuckoos are crying.

To a Certain Unmarried Woman

A woman became naked. But
not to wait for caresses.

In transient daylight
the faint scent of skin.
Fine wrinkles
of the thin flowerpetals
of a woman who has not known sensuality.

Like bruises that are ripe,
smears of light blue color,
those marks which remain all over her body
are traces of fingers of the people who touched her
    passing by.
The same as unsold fruit
at the shop-front of a fruit store.

A woman became naked. Just for a while
to change a summer dress into an autumn dress.

Recitative—A Lakeshore Poem

Shutting my eyes, secretly I have
come to escape
to the shores of this lake
where even fingertips are dyed an intense blue.

The lakeshore's landscape
is precipitous with crystals.
Among the frozen rockeries are stirring
young goats.

Mountain after mountain darkens, with
mottled snow,
mountain after mountain shines, like
rosy wine.

Without being pursued by the hurry of time,
as though just making smoke
the days have moved along
swaying like shadows of jewel-balls.

I came so I could walk upon the snowy path
where turtledoves cry in the forest of larch trees
and be away from the rough-hearted people
who both day and night give themselves to the war.

In the solitary way of one going blind,
at the side of the lake frozen all over with ice, day after day
I come to stand for a while
as though arrived there in a dream.

My spirit rising and rising rebelliously,
my poetry afraid of being seen,
close to purified death, the eternal hand,
are to be buried in ice until next spring.

I have come to escape
from that spiritual poverty
and from the unreasonable
hunting-out.

Separating from feeble friends
who have forgotten to be critical,
leaving loved rooms
where I slept and arose for months and years.

Everything will turn into bones and ashes
because of the stupidity of human beings who forget human
    beings.
My moans of suffering come from this too.
The lights fade away. All around is an empty commotion.

Snowflakes fall from high branches of trees.
Withered bush-clover rustles.
Underneath the thick ice
dead water blows on a *dōshō*.*

And then the glittering stars' animated
nighttime,
the enchased heavens'
unfeeling spectacle!

* A wind instrument of ancient China

Mount Fuji

The same as stacked lunchboxes
this Japan, narrow and confined.

From this corner to that corner, meanly and stingily
all of us are being counted up.
And, unlimited rudeness,
all of us are drafted—stupid idiots.

Birth certificates, they ought to be burned right away.
Nobody should remember my son.

My son,
be concealed away inside this hand.
Hide away for a while underneath a hat.

Both your father and mother in the house at the foot of
   the mountain
have talked about it all night long.

Soaking the withered forest at the foot of the mountain,
making sounds like twigs breaking, crackle, crackle,
the whole night rain was falling.

My son, you are soaked wet to the skin
carrying a heavy gun, gasping for breath,
walking along as if fallen into a trance. What place is it?

That place is not known. But for you
both your father and mother go outside to search
   aimlessly.

The night hateful with only such dreams,
the long anxious nighttime, at last ends.

The rain has let up.
In the sky vacant without my son,
well, how damnably disgusting,
like a shabby worn-out bathrobe,
Fuji!

❧

SHIGEJI TSUBOI
(b. 1898)

壺
井
繁
治

River of Ice

Watching scarce flowers
the day grows dark.

Around the flowers
air becomes more and more cold,
not even a moth appears now.

No letter from anywhere,
autumn nights
the sound of insects
flows like water.

What is the sound of insects crying through the night
    seeking for?
Into me it comes flowing,
finally turns to a river of ice.

Night Skylark

Burning from the bottle of the earth,
roots,
leaves,
stems,
ears,
all toward the sky.
As far as one can see,
continuously burning, the wheat field's big fire.

A night skylark
without a place to land
sings infinitely in the height of the sky.

You, the one that was judged last,
presently
will fall down into the sea of fire.

Sunflower

O sunflower,
flame that is born from flame,
explosion into the sun . . .

Cable Cars

Deep at the bottom of a precipice
a swift stream intensely blue goes bubbling by,
in the unlimited sky beyond
a cable car moves along
burdened by a load that is heavy
and unseen by eyes.
Its thick cable
might be cut off at any unknown time.

Inside myself also
something continually keeps moving along.
Possibly
it might be an express train.

The middle of the night . . .
though almost all noises have faded away,
in the ears' intensely dark tunnel
there is something hurrying through.

Danger!
Unconsciously shouting,
my own voice awakens me,
the one eye of an intensely red signal
keeps staring at me.

From morning
until late at night
time is regulated by stop-go signals.

Danger!
Larger than an infant's head,
a single egg
comes rolling down from somewhere
and crosses the street. . . .

Inside the intense darkness
now again
cable cars
are seen to be crossing.

For the sake of public construction work,
I thought, maybe, they were loaded
full of cement,
but with skeletons only
the cable cars were loaded,
one after another
endlessly moving away.

Balloon

Faced toward the sky
an immense yawn was given, and then
from the inside of a mouth
a single balloon came popping out.
As it ascended up and up to the sky
gradually it expanded to a hugeness.

Its interior
is completely filled with poison gas
and we cannot tell when it will explode—
that kind of a rumor spread throughout the entire city.

Covering a small
city's sky,
the enormous balloon.
From the morning until the night it
dingle-dangled about like a ghost.

This city's population
completely tired of living,
in the sky
even the sun's existence had been forgotten. But
at the balloon's appearance, with fear and trembling
they look up at the sky all the time.

When
and what kind of accident will happen cannot be known so
the entire city
developed more hubbub than a revolution.

Into every direction the police
dispatched detectives, but
the important criminal was not discovered any place at all.

—Please report if you see the man who gave the yawn!
—Also as many details as possible about the man's
   appearance!
Although such assistance was desired from the city's
   population,
a man who is yawning
is far too common and
which was the genuine criminal couldn't be learned.

In spite of their reputation
the police were worn out by it all.

And now still
above that small city's roofs
the balloon
dingle-dangles about the same as ever.
At the whim of the blowing wind,
to the west,
to the east . . .

Bear

Although it is the middle of March
this morning there is an unusual heavy snowfall.
With high boots
walking in the snow, crunch, crunch,
goodness how huge my own footprints!
Right in Tokyo I turned into a bear.
Aren't there any human beings!
Isn't there a creature called a human being?

Motionless Night

This night that is dark and cold does not move.
My eyes, and my beating heart,
and charming flowers, and smiles, do not exist.
Wind blows inside the being that is unable to sleep.
At midnight the table-clock stops.
I feel reluctant to wind its springs
in this hollow room
where I am alone and
without any miracle happening
the night continues to deepen.

❧

YOSHIAKI SASAZAWA
(b. 1898)

笹
沢
美
明

Flowers of June

In the wet season,
under shadows of green leaves, wind heavily
pauses, bewildered and tired.
In such a season
in the hospital garden conversation gets wet
. . . "How are you feeling?" . . .
. . . "Well, not too fine." . . .
Only flowers, as though resisting this wetness,
are standing dry,
flowers of poppy, windflowers, and others.
After rain, in space between clouds, shining in blue sky,
hollyhocks stand near a hedge.
Deep red and golden, vigorous flowers of midsummer
preluding a season.
Wet wind is made to flow lightly
by flowers of June.

The Tower

It is not a hand that stretches up toward Paradise.
Neither is it a symbol of the spirit of civilization's science.
Is it an arrow sign for the sake of the future
of human beings escaping
from a large city whose civilization is beginning to decay
　and decompose?
In order to pierce through and spoil the skin of space,
is it a boring?
From its sharp tip again today
the light flashes and leaps out.

SHINJIRŌ KURAHARA
(1889–1965)

蔵原伸二郎

The Fox

The fox realizes tha·
in this desolate sunbright field
there is only him alone.
That because of this he himself is a part of the field,
that he is the whole of it.
To turn into the wind too, to turn into the dried grasses
    too,
and even to turn into a streak of light too
inside the fox-colored desolate field,
almost like existing or not existing,
is being like a shadow, that too he realizes.
He realizes how to run almost like the wind too, to run
    even quicker than light too.
Because of this he believes that his figure is invisible to
    anybody.
A thing that is invisible is running while thinking.
A thought alone is running.
Without anyone being aware of it the midday moon has
    risen above the desolate field.

A Secret Code

I wonder what thing that is coming out in opposition to
  time.
A secret code from the future.
It is however not that of a human being,
and of course not either from anything like a god, whose
  existence cannot be imagined.

Over there on the desert
underneath the non-objective sky which is drying up bit
  by bit,
clinging to the one single blade of grass that is left on
  earth,
it is the last butterfly sending up a signal.

Footprints

A thing of a time long ago,
a fox was running along on the clay surface of a river bank.
After that
several tens of thousands of years passed by,
that clay surface became fossil, the footprints are still there.
If the footprints are seen, then what the fox was thinking
  while running can be understood.

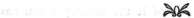

TATSUJI MIYOSHI
(1900–1964)

三好達治

Lake Water

Inside the water of this lake a person has passed away
and because of it so many boats are out there.

Among reeds and water weeds—where has the body
   been hidden?
The fife-signal of finding it has not been sounded yet.

A wind is blowing—the sound of oars cutting through the
   water, the sound of paddles.
A wind is blowing—the smell of grass roots and crabs is
   here.

Oh who is it that could be sure?
Inside the water of this lake a person passed away at
   dawn?

Who is it that actually could be sure
although already the night has become this late?

A Boy

At evening
from the gate of a certain temple
a handsome little boy is coming back.

At the day which is about to darken
tossing a handball,
tossing a handball high up toward the sky,
still playing, he is coming back.

On the tranquil street
both people and trees make the air calm
and the sky is flowing along in the way of a dream.

Snow Bunting

At this division in the road where day darkens the sleigh
    has started . . .
Behind the stopping place a snow bunting is crying and
    singing.
Over the snow where dusk gathers it is crying and singing.
On the twig of a leafless tree, ah it is burning, a single
    song, a single life.

Golden Venus

In a sealike evening sky
a golden honeybee makes wing sounds
like buzzing ears. . . .

On the other side of the valley
by the mountain opposite,
poised on top of the thin forest—Venus.

Presently that woman is hidden by a ridge.
I climb up onto a rock.
For a while she is visible.

Presently that woman is hidden by a ridge.
I get up onto a hilltop.
For a while she is visible.

That woman vanishes. That woman goes down.
That woman goes down. She goes away.
Earth is warped. . . . The mountain tilts. . . .

Great Aso*

Horses are standing in rain.
A herd of horses with one or two foals is standing in rain.
In hushed silence rain is falling.
The horses are eating grass.
With tails, and backs too, and manes too, completely soaking wet
they are eating grass,
eating grass.
Some of them are standing with necks bowed over absent-mindedly and not eating grass.
Rain is falling and falling in hushed silence.
The mountain is sending up smoke.
The peak of Nakadake is sending up dimly yellowish and heavily oppressive volcanic smoke, densely, densely.
And rain clouds too all over the sky.
Still they continue without ending.
Horses are eating grass.
On one of the hills of the Thousand-Mile-Shore-of-Grass
they are absorbedly eating blue-green grass.
Eating.
They are all standing there quietly.
They are quietly gathered in one place forever, dripping and soaked with rain.
If a hundred years go by in this single moment, there would be no wonder.
Rain is falling. Rain is falling.
In hushed silence rain is falling.

* The volcano crater

Over the Paving Stones

Oh sad, flower petals drift down,
onto the young girls flower petals drift down,
young girls quietly talking as they walk,
the sound of serene footsteps drifting into the sky,
occasionally raising their eyes
they pass by the springtime in a shadeless temple garden.
The tiled roof of the temple has turned green
and at each of its eaves
the wind bells are hanging silent while
being alone
I let my own shadow walk over the paving stones.

The Deer

In the morning in a forest a deer is crouching.
Upon his shoulders, the shadow of his horns.
A single deerfly cuts across the space of the breeze and
    hovers
close to his ears as they listen to a far-off river valley.

FUYUHIKO KITAGAWA
(b. 1900)

北
川
冬
彦

Face

The harbor was
bright like midday with the wetness of the full moon.
Wind from the open sea
came along bearing strange faces.
Faces appear one after another, numerously.
Pale white faces that cannot seem alive.
Faces that forgot to get angry or to curse.
Faces
appear and disappear,
disappear and appear.
Ah,
sorrow that the passing faces endure, deep deep sorrow.
This sorrow cannot help infiltrate
into every corner
of this country.

Bubbles

From the stagnated river's
reeds
roots, bubbling bubbling, come rising to the surface
bubbles.

Those bubbles, each one, each one,
inside blurred spheres,
although they contain abundant discontent, dissatisfaction,
on the water surface
they are transient, disappear, and are gone.

At night
bubbles
at the river bottom
lie dormant in the midst of muddy earth, but
when midday comes
dim rays of light shine into them and
carelessly, absently, they come rising up.

Deception's light!
Those hands!
Being tempted,
the river bottom's dark dark world—
Although down there is the dwelling place of bubbles,
although down there is where it is their merit to expand
    fully their surface tensions.

Weeds

Weeds
paying no attention to surroundings
are growing as they want to grow.
This scenery gives a feeling of contentment.
Although stepped on by people,
before we can be aware,
they have lengthened so much that one's knees are hidden.
In some places
even a person's body is lost from sight
there are such deep places.
This scenery gives a feeling of contentment.
When able to grow without limit
they should go ahead and spread out.
Even though not attractive
the plentiful flowers should open abundantly.

SHIRŌ MURANO
(b. 1901)

Diving

I come walking out from inside a white cloud,
out to the tip of one board's length.
I bend over very far.
Time gets wrinkled up to there.
Kick! I have kicked.
Inside the sky already!
The sky continues holding me.
Muscles are hooked to the sky,
but they fall off.
Chased, pierced!
I struggle inside a sensation of transparency.
Outside the bubbles above my head
women's laughter and waists appear.
A red beach umbrella's
big stripes I hurry to grab.

Grave Visiting*

Though that sea which is called Solomon's
direction is unknown,
the body which was submerged there
sleeps in Musashino's ground.
This civilization which is impossible to understand
is extremely difficult for me to endure.

Anyway I
riding on a painted electric train
have come all the way,
and was reading Camus in the car.
Among the dried grasses
violets are out, their purple.
On the rocks the fruit of wild roses
lies darkened like water drops of recollection.

Oh forever is a transparent stomach.
Bones, nature,
are they only its feces?
Everywhere the great excretion of spring.
And yet within it,
undigested, the dubiousness of human beings.
For the sake of a shriveled-up mummy
I
pray a long time.

* At Musashino

Horse on a City Street

Horse!
Big naked primitive
with blue organs inside!
He often
slipped on the polished artificial marble.
With teeth exposed, he looked back, but
nobody was there.

Poor raw-smelling spirit
that strayed into a peculiar country!
Here
is a transparent hell
where everything evaporates.
First death too,
second death too,
and even the myth.

The horse
recognized a mystic sign
at a strange city corner—
his race's eternal transmigration,
that intense red Pegasus.

On Suicide

My memory is
redder than meat at a meat market and
my past is
like flower patterns on porcelain
accurate and at the same time minute in the extreme.
But still this condition of debility,
comes from what kind of reason?

Quietly putting the muzzle to my temple
I try to pull the trigger.
Sour candy goes through my insides and then
from the shelf behind one
ornament tumbles down.
That is all,
just that is all!—
from a world's tiny broken hole
yellow smoke is coming up.

Is life after all
a remote remote lyrical hardening, is it?
But almost the same are
odds and ends of broken toys
wrapped in a big bundle in a cloth
and like this as abruptly tumbled over.

No one comes like a perpetual undertaker.
After time elapses the lock is opened
and another cloth-wrapped bundle comes to just look in.

A Small Bird's Sky
(a song)

Inside your big breast
our songs frolic.
But when nighttime comes
you do not keep me.
You have no bed of twigs to let me stay on.
I grieve because of this.
I will sleep in the earth's night of fangs and claws.

The color of milk,
your breast is warm.
But when I have been struck down
you do not enfold me.
The weight of even such a tiny sin
you do not have enough strength to hold up.
I grieve because of this.
I fall down and on the freezing earth rot away.

Night Storm

I casually stop my midnight writing.
From somewhere a man's voice was heard.
Too, I feel I could hear the whistling of my brother who
    supposedly was killed in a sea battle.

But they
of course must have come from my imagining ears.
Outside, reverberating through the darkness,
a night storm is blowing harder.
Crazily dancing, the garden trees rustle.
Violent at times
is the wind's blowing sound in the bamboo hedge.

This seasonal wind
flows across the southern islands
blowing on all of the injuries of our world,
eventually flows across the continent,
and will run away to the vastness of far-off Siberia.
But even so, in the middle of this commotion,
certainly
there are and should be numerous voices.
I believe there are and should be tidings that are hand to
    tell.

I strain my intent ears.
Then suddenly, boisterously,
combined with the noise of the door of an abandoned
    greenhouse falling down

is heard the scream of shattering glass.
Because of my horror I
unexpectedly drop my pen.
An invisible current of air whirls around me and
　　passes away—
soon, alone, I laugh at myself
and resume writing my new essay on poetry.

I am sure tomorrow
upon the blown-out morning sky,
with so much whiteness they hurt my forehead,
popping, the plum blossoms might open up.

A Deer

A deer at the verge of the forest
in the sunset was standing motionless.
He knew
his small forehead was being aimed at
nevertheless for him
what was there to do?
He, standing elegantly,
was staring toward a village
(the time for living glistens like gold)
from there where his dwelling place was
against the night of the big forest.

The Bridge

At night in the city
from thousands of wounds
blood comes spurting out.

It comes flowing into the canal
that is stagnant, dully,
where the bridge is suspended.
The bridge is neither going toward a future
nor coming from a past,
just from the opposite shore, to this shore,
it is only hanging
over a dead current
and just fastening together two nights.

When night becomes late, over there at its top
an aged man and a young woman come
and, without appearing confident,
casually hug one another.

The Canal at Night

From somewhere, half asleep, a seagull cries out.
A small fish that has swallowed tar
from time to time tormentedly leaps up
and in the same way goes down under the waves again.

This place is not an ocean.
With no origin, without an outlet.
The bottom of night, a river without a name.
Destiny is motionless,
destiny's river.
Inside a warmish mist
smelling of a horse's odor
a blood-filled lamp shines all night long,
and out of the shade, totteringly,
a person from the past comes staggering,
augh, pours out quantities of vomit.

At the bottom of human consciousness
the backed-up waters of sin without an outlet,
sleeping, that tender river.

The Ox

Glittering eyelashes and behind them
the meek eyeballs of dreaminess
that almost become invisible.
And there around the artless brow
an abundance of golden hair is curling.

Past this expression that has no future
the thing that is crouching heavily
with its black weight
is a large "now."

A young couple who will be married
keep watching him for a long time
and wonder about life
while against a narrow flexible-looking
white fence they are leaning.

SHINKICHI TAKAHASHI
(b. 1901)

高橋新吉

Broken Glasses

Petals of chrysanthemums have been burnt by flames
   and blackly scorched.
Inside the roaring sounds of the city's commotion
fragrance has faded away.

The slaughter keeps on continuously.
The bombs of the bombing planes
are released like waterfalls.

Immature books have been blasted away,
superfluous desires have been burnt out,
the ground is completely filling with poisonous gases.

Amongst the accumulated smells of rotting
there is only one thing that is not at all shaken,
an abandoned pair of glasses.

The Fly

I thought I would live forever.
Forever was inside a single fly.

When the fly was chased by a hand
he flew away gently.
Toward that attitude of composure
I felt friendliness.

Late at night
with the electric light shining,
listening to the sounds of rain outside,
I was reading a book.

On a page of the opened book
a single fly
cast a shadow of loneliness without realizing it.

Forever, like a fly's legs, is
thinly bending.

The Ocean

The ocean was bottomlessly deep.
Standing at the edge of the ocean
I looked toward the bottom of the ocean.

Dangerously near tumbling off,
what I thought of was the things of my future.
Time was imagined like the legs of an infant who has not
    yet walked.

No matter what happens anywhere
there is nothing else to do
but stand on this steep cliff, clench my teeth, and close
    my eyes.

The unexperienced future
like fishermen's fires flickering past the horizon
has darkness around itself.

I seem to have thrown my body down into that ocean.

IKU TAKENAKA
(b. 1904)

竹
中
郁

Despair

I am sleeping
together with someone
in a single bed.

An affectionate arm-pillow is loaned to me.
I fondle only that arm.

Except for that
no body,
no face,
no hair.

Who do you think the person is?
Guess please.

Stars at Night

There are stars above Japan.
There are stars that smell of gasoline.
There are stars that have heavy accents.
There are stars that sound like Ford automobiles.
There are stars that are Coca Cola colored.
There are stars that have the humming of electric
    refrigerators.
There are stars that contain the rattling of cans.

Cleaned out with gauze and pincers
there are stars disinfected with formalin.
There are stars that hold radioactivity.
Among the stars are some too quick to catch with the eyes.
Stars that run along unexpected orbits.
Deeply, deeply,
stars are seen too that thrust into the gorge-bottom of the
    universe.

There are stars up above Japan.
They, on a winter's night,
each night, each night,
are seen linked like heavy chains.

SEI ITŌ
(1905–1969)

伊
藤
整

Melancholy Summer

Already I—have become tired of such a deep-colored
    summer.
In the grove the masses of royal fern—have grown up to
    their full height and
underneath them
I suppose such things as beetles, frogs, and blue-green
    dwarves are walking.
This greenness like a sea
must have totally dyed the expression of my eyes.
Turtledoves also
in the forest depths
are very sleepily crying.
Swaying trees are turning over leaves to whiteness,
a wagon even—could not be seen going rattling above the
    valley.
The sky has cleared up entirely and,
with not even one memory to enliven my heart,

quickly
this summer will go away and
oh when will a time come
when a surprising thing will happen in my universe?
Until then
even if it is for years and years I
will keep on having a dream impossible to tell.
Girls who were friends of earlier days
all—know love or are pallid wives of others.
And so—I at eighteen—I at nineteen,
being left a solitary retreating figure,
into the forest-depths of the needle-dropping pine trees
    disappeared.

A Night Frozen Hard

A cat is wailing.
On the road through the snow a child walked along
    shedding tears.
The sky was filled with the glitter of stars.
Snow was frozen hard.
Next door the bride, suffering after childbirth,
lay in bed with swollen cheeks.
You cat! Don't cry so stubbornly and terribly.
Again tonight it is so silent that
on the road through the snow several kinds of creatures
    are walking around.

A Night of the Moon Again

Under the light of this moon
I probably will go walking on and on unconscious of where.
Ah, on my hands and the long grasses
soft tender light is being reflected the same as phosphorus.
It seems I am not alone.
It seems I go walking with someone, such a bright path.
It is so beautiful that
I want to hold the light in my hands and look at it.
If we should meet inside such moonlight,
without saying anything she
would probably come following after me
and it would probably become clear we both told lies.

SHIZUO ITŌ
(1906–1953)

Watching the Beam of a Lighthouse

On the dark sea the green beam from a lighthouse.
What tenderness.
Blinking, turning around
in my night,
the whole night, it wanders.

And you
to my night
give many many meanings
of grief and wishes
that cannot be told.

O griefs, wishes, and what tenderness.
Though nothing exists,
in my night,
the whole night
the green beam from a lighthouse wanders.

Locusts in the Garden

After my journey
here in this garden the garden locusts were crying.
I wanted to write
something like a poem.
Paper open,
like water, plain, several lines came out
and then
in front of what was written,
unexpectedly, utterly different from it
and with a kind of sense of a previous life,
with a sickly feeling accompanied by faint dizziness,
I was hearing the locusts.

JUN TAKAMI
(1907–1965)

高見順

At the Boundary of Life and Death

At the boundary of life and death
what exists I wonder?
For instance, concerning the boundary of country and
    country,
during the war, on the border of Thailand and Burma,
although I saw it when I crossed through the jungle,
nothing unusual was found at that place.
There was nothing like a boundary line drawn.
Also at sea when passing directly over the equator
nothing special like a beacon mark was visible.
No, at that place was the wonderful dark blue sea.
On the Thailand-Burma border was a wonderful sky.
After a squall a wonderful rainbow hung in the sky.
On the life-death boundary too might there not be
    something hung like a wonderful rainbow,
even though my surroundings
and also my self
were a devastated jungle?

Fingernails of the Dead

Upon cold bricks
ivy lengthens.
At the bottom of night
time accumulates heavily,
fingernails of the dead lengthen.

TSUNAO AIDA
(b. 1914)

会
田
綱
雄

Wild Duck

"Do not become a duck!"
At the time,
was that what the duck said?

No.

We plucked feathers,
singed down,
roasted the meat and gobbled it up. All of us
licking and licking our lips,
an evening haze hanging over the edge of the swamp
we were leaving. It was then.

"Wait, wait,
the bones can still be sucked on!"

We all looked back
and the duck's laughing and
glittering keel of bones was seen.

Legend

From the lakewater,
when a crab comes crawling out
together we tie it up with a string
and go over the mountain,
at the market
stand on a road covered with pebbles.

There are people who eat crabs!

Dangled from a string,
with ten legs with hair growing on them
scratching at the sky,
the crab changes into money,
together we buy a handful of rice and salt
and go over the mountain
to return to the lakewater shore.

At this place
the grass is withered,
the wind is freezing,
the hut where we live together does not have a lamp to
    light.

Inside in the darkness together we,
over and over again,
over and over again,
tell to the children we together have
memories of the fathers and mothers we together had.
Fathers and mothers we together had also,

like we do together,
caught crabs from this lakewater,
went over that mountain,
brought back a handful of rice and salt,
and for the sake of us together
they cooked a supper of hot gruel.

Some day again we together,
just as the fathers and mothers we together had,
softly,
softly,
will go to the lakewater and cast aside
small thin-weak bodies.
And the cast-off shells we together had
crabs will eat up without leaving any bits.
Just as a long time ago
the cast-off shells of the fathers and mothers we
   together had
were eaten up without leaving any bits.

It is the unfulfilled desire we together have.

When the children go to sleep
together we slip out of the hut,
set a boat adrift on the lakewater.
On the lakewater it is dimly lighted
and shivering together we
tenderly,
painfully,
love each other.

MINORU YOSHIOKA
(b. 1919)

吉岡

実

Egg

A time when even the gods are absent,
not even shadows of living things exist,
not even the smell of death is ascending,
a summer afternoon of deep prostration.
From a congested area,
tearing off cloudlike things,
inundating things of stickiness,
at a place completely deserted
there is a thing that originates.
There is a thing that suggests a life,
polished by dust and light
one single egg that is occupying the grand earth.

Still Life

Inside the rigid-surfaced bowl of the night,
increasing vividness,
autumn fruit.
Apple and pear and grape varieties,
every one of them,
piled up as they are in a pose
in sleeping
in a unified harmony,
enter into magnificent music.
Each one's deepest place having been reached into,
cores leisurely lay themselves down.
Around them
circles an abundant time of rotting.
Now in front of the dead's teeth,
like rocks with nothing coming out of them,
those varieties of fruit
more and more increase their weight.
And within the deep bowl,
inside an apparition of this night,
eventually,
lean far over.

A Funeral Piece

I am a person who has drowned,
a single individual's
sack of collapsing time, am that fact.
I wonder who verifies it now,
the long time of submerging,
the long journey's end
without the sun
or clouds flying in the evening glow,
without hearing the low voices of couples at street corners.

My mouth that has no shape is murmuring.
The bubbles of my voice are in vain.
My eyes that have no shape see
that jellyfish, innumerable like stars, go ascending quietly
    quietly.
Dimly ignited
microscopic eyes of jellyfish
all at the same time take a look
at my load that is sinking down.
For that time it seems as if there were months and years
    of awful silence.

The testifiers of my death,
are they those swarms of jellyfish?
Or, excessively stroking my private parts,
are they the tentacles of kinds of seaweeds?

Or, so I can be accepted
and my situation be placed,
are they the horizontal reefs
put in darkness more deeply
farther away?

The load was brought from the land.
Around the sack whose contents have been completely
    emptied out
are numerous worlds,
numerous pasts and futures,
numerous excesses and poverties of existence.
Stepping over them all
comes the magnitude of my death,
that quiet wholeness.

Trailing around the half-decomposed body
several thousands of varieties of fish are swimming.

SABURŌ KURODA
(b. 1919)

黒
田
三
郎

The Sea

Running out
crying
laughing
whirling my arms
kicking back sand
a domesticated
little being
to wild nature
the sea
returns

Nature

Nature
tells everything in silence
to one that passes by busily
the voice is inaudible
a far green cape
sand over a fence
that's all

Hide and Seek

Suddenly still
the world becomes quiet

Everyone wickedly
becomes silent

By a downy cheek
a half-warm wind blows

HITOSHI ANZAI
(b. 1919)

安
西
均

The Discarded Horse

What on earth is it, going from where to where,
that is passing around through here I wonder?
The same as a wounded god,
a single abandoned military horse.
Shining more than death,
alone more than liberty,
and at the same time like peacefulness without a helper,
is the field of snow where he temporarily wanders about
with hardly his own lean shadow to feed on.
Presently one cry is neighed-out toward the distance
and collapsing from the knees he has tumbled down.
The Asian snow, the heavenly evening!

The Flower Shop

On a solitary night, vaguely coloring a certain street corner,
a flower shop is full of flowers like animated words.

It is pleasant to look for flowers when melancholy.
It is even better, while smiling, to give those flowers to
someone.

But even more than that, instead of looking for flowers
to give
it is best to watch flowers while discarding the many
selves.

At the flower shop my words too are various like animated
flowers.
When I turn the street corner at night my being is again
one thing,

just a being in distress, that can see everything.

MASAO NAKAGIRI
(b. 1919)

中
桐
雅
夫

The Electric Train

A person hanging onto a strap!
A person sitting upon a seat!
A person swaying in time to the sway!
Under the gloomy electric lights,
who you are nobody knows
getting off at your station.
There are times of riding beyond the station and coming
 back again.
Who you are even you do not know.

Your exhausted necktie—
inside of its knot
something you do not realize is hiding.
Broken-down shoes unpolished for how-many days—
inside the worn-out leather heels
something that irritates you is hiding.
If you think it over well
you will come to realize what it is.

It is hiding inside the flame of a single match
burning your dead body.

NOBUO AYUKAWA
(b. 1920)

鮎
川
信
夫

The Evening Sun

The roof above the tops of the summer weeds becomes
    entirely hidden.
Though until just now children were sticking their faces
    from the doorway
they have all become invisible.
At my back
the town gradually becomes smaller.
Everything everywhere is no more than the play of lights
    and shadows.
Insects are crying with thin voices.
For what reason do they keep on going from the beginning
    again
although it would be better for them to be quiet in a corner
    of memory?

Now I will climb a hill.
If only this summer will pass,
the cool wind come blowing again
and comfort my feelings, but . . .

Chasing after the sky, coming up to here,
this cannot be called a hill anymore.
It is as though from an even higher elevation
I dropped into the depths of the still higher blue sky,
the deepest blue sky.

This is exhilarating, even to me.
Both close and distant, was there ever such an evening sun
   going down?

Leaving Harbor

It was a morning of quietness.
All of the anchor chains broke off by themselves,
all of the ships seemed to be going out from the harbor,
it was a morning of loveliness.

Standing on the deck
with a newly made friend and our arms on each other's
   shoulders,
I was seeing far off with the strained eyes of a seagull
the lifted green froth of the palm forest
disappear into the rising mist from the water.
(Already I cannot remember that friend's name.)

Being out on the sea like that
long days and months go by in a twinkling.
(Already I have forgotten the things of that year.)

Look! Blown about by the wind!
In what way can we
turn into wings that are white and buoyant?

Ah, without any difference between night and day,
in the vast heavens we uselessly
were seeking for a single island.
Around the Southern Cross
the bow of the ship with its life preserver
just continues circling about indefinitely.

A Wanderer

Cliffs break off,
on the slopes dried grasses might be swaying,
in the open views that are here and there
electric wires might be humming.
Standing on the outskirts of cities that are like that
it is strange how unexpectedly good a puff of tobacco.

Underneath the moon of midday
just a neglected road continues on.
Sometimes a single man
approaches the place from far away.
And by only that

the earth's autumn seems to be deepened.
Only a man who comes walking along a lonely road
can really feel the threats of this coldness like an
   aristocrat's.

Everything is passed,
but even at a moment of going by in silence
what fascinations are to be found.
A man wearing a black suit of mourning,
on his bluish pale forehead sorrow
and a tiny whorl of curly hair, for example, might be
   discovered.

RYŪICHI TAMURA
(b. 1923)

Four Thousand Days and Nights

In order for a single poem to come into existence,
you and I have to kill,
have to kill many things,
many lovable things, kill by shooting, kill by assassination,
  kill by poisoning.

Look!
Out of the sky of four thousand days and nights,
just because we wanted the trembling tongue of one
  small bird,
four thousand nights of silence and four thousand days
  of counterlight
you and I killed by shooting.

Listen!
Out of all the cities of falling rain, smelting furnaces,
midsummer harbors, and coal mines,
just because we needed the tears of a single hungry child

four thousand days of love and four thousand nights of
  compassion
you and I killed by assassination.

Remember!
Just because we wanted the fear of one vagrant dog
who could see the things you and I couldn't see with our
  eyes
and could hear the things you and I couldn't hear with our
  ears,
four thousand nights of imagination and four thousand days
  of chilling recollection
you and I killed by poison.

In order for a single poem to come
you and I have to kill beloved things.
This is the only way to bring back the dead to life.
You and I have to follow that way.

TARŌ YAMAMOTO
(b. 1925)

山本太郎

from "Journey"

Astride a Himalayan pony
I pass through a forest of orchids.
I am wanting to meet Maya-bunin.
This journey—unexpectedly
is a varied dining table—full of shuddering.
Under the shadow of pagoda trees
I sit in a tea shop made of pure mud
and take off—my face
and wipe accumulated years of sweat.
On the highway—shimmering air.
Small boys—limbs and bodies
being scattered
swim away in the midst of light.

In a Surgery Room

The baby's stomach on the inside
with flower petals was fully stuffed;
made transparent by the rays from a skylight,
like a meadow of flowers they were swaying.
Such things as a minute butterfly's dead body
showed faintly, a quiet garden it was.
When the stomach was open, flower petals
turned into red goldfish began swimming.
Right before the baby's protruding eyes
the mask of the doctor,
the same as adhesive tape, was mirrored.

Outside the cold wind of winter was.
In the baby's eyes
a light seemed to have puffed out.
The sweet breath of sleep could be heard, yet
could not be heard.
The baby certainly was sleeping.
Ah, that was the sound of a swayed curtain.
Like a minute blue vase,
the baby's spirit slipped through it,
back to a faraway country returning.

SHUNTARŌ TANIKAWA
(b. 1931)

谷川俊太郎

Growth

At three
I didn't have a past

At five
my past was to yesterday

At seven
my past was to the age of warriors

At eleven
my past was to dinosaurs

At fourteen
my past was as the textbooks

At sixteen
I watched the infinity of the past with fear

At eighteen
I don't know what time is

The Hospital

Blue sky and sun are dissolved in stained creosote water,
in dark corridors eroded emotions accumulate rather than
   science.

Bright-colored suits are powerless in front of X rays.
Even in white clothes there is no consolation.

When patients
into the bottoms of test tubes of colored glass
timidly confine their own being
white physicians
becoming cool and accurate machines
handle cool and accurate machines.

Inside the several kinds of reverberations I do not hear
   a human voice.
In here everything is materialism.

The hospital is the same as a modern city without secrets.

The Kiss

As eyes are closing the world goes away,
only the weight of tenderness assures me infinitely. . . .

Silence turns into a quiet night
encircling us like a promise,
it now is not an estranging thing,

rather a tender farness that surrounds us
so therefor we by chance become lonely. . . .

We search together
in a way that is more certain than to speak or look
and we discover
when we lose ourselves—

I wonder what I wanted to assure;
tenderness which returned from a long way off.
Losing words in purified silence
you now only just breathing.

You indeed now are life itself. . . .
but even these words are punishable
presently when tenderness fills the world
and I fall down so I may live in it.

Distress

By the place where the sound of the blue sky's waves is
    heard
I feel that I might have
lost something terribly important.

At the station of the transparent past
when I stand in front of the lost-and-found counter
I have become even more distressed.

Picnic to the Earth

Here let's jump rope together, here.
Here let's eat rice balls together.
Here I will love you.
Your eyes reflect the blue of the sky.
Your back will be dyed with the green of the herbs.
Here we will learn the names of the stars together.

Staying here let's imagine all the things that are far off.
Here let's gather seashells.
From the sea of the daybreak's sky
let's bring back tiny starfish.
At breakfast we will throw them out
and let the night go away.

Here I will keep on saying "I have returned!"
as long as you repeat "Welcome back!"
Here I will keep on returning to again and again.
Here let's drink hot tea.
Here sitting together for a while
let's have the refreshing wind touching us.

MAKOTO ŌOKA
(b. 1931)

大
岡
信

To Live

I wonder if people know
that there are several layers in the water?
Fish deep in it and duckweed drifting on its surface
bathe in different lights.
That makes them various colored.
That gives them shadows.

I gather up pearls on a pavement.
I live inside a phantom forest;
upon notes of music scattered over the strings of my being.
I live in hollows of drops that trickle upon snow;
in damp ground of morning where liverwort opens.
I live upon a map of the past and future.

I have forgotten the color my eyes were yesterday.
But what things my eyes saw yesterday
my fingers realize
because what eyes saw was by hands
patted like touching the bark of a beech tree.
O I live upon sensations blown about by wind.

Without One Particle of Sentiment in His Being

A fellow who does not have even one particle of sentiment
    in his being
goes across the Sumida River in winter
toward the universe without love
and without a bird.

A fellow who does not have even one particle of courage
    in his being
is filling his lungs with tar
and washing a child's neck
in the Sumida River where the desperate evening sun
    overflows.

I made a long journey
on a distant way that could not be accounted for during
    thirty years
together with toppled-down women
all by myself.

What I am attempting to approach
is perhaps made of wind,
an elusive and invisible city.
It is a city of the pain of a man beginning to bear a child.

For me to believe in the conqueror's goodwill
or the deceived class's
heartfelt evil-will to believe in is not possible.

For heaven's sake, at least,
the innocence that is going to be born,
don't touch it, anyone!

ATSUHIRO SAWAI
(b. 1940)

沢井淳弘

An Occasional Image

Casually curving on a country road,
facing toward an utterly different view—
the same mental image of the past,
where was it,
when was it?
The time and also the place, not exact,
pass over my consciousness at certain moments.

Strangely clear
that scenery of the mind,
a thing awaking in a fathomless place,
a being always observing the thoughts of my self,
the impulse inside my self,
a view-point of the bird's eye,
my self that is not my self.

Early Spring

If I make an attempt to walk with each and every thing
    thrown off
the air with the mischievous smile of a devil
attempts to present all things to me
so that my being will be bewitched by any one of them.

I throw them away
and then I begin to walk all over again.
And the world is in early spring.
Under the girdered expressway a milk-colored haze is
    hanging,
the sunlight of morning shining into it aslant.

Where a powdering of frost halfway comes off the tops
    of roofs
children of sunlight blow upon tiny horns of spring.
Heads of grey-green colored hills and
heads of buildings on this side stretch up billowingly.

Looking out on this scene of such joyful existence
now I will stop questioning the condition of "happiness."

If I make an attempt to walk with each and every thing
   thrown off
the air with the mischievous smile of a devil
   attempts to present all things to me
so that my being will be bewitched by any one of them.

   I throw them away,
 and then I begin to walk all over again.
   And the world is in early spring.
Under the painted expressway a milk-colored haze is
   hanging,
 the sunlight of morning shining into it colors.
Where a pondering of frost softly takes off the tops
   of roofs
 chills of sunlight blow upon tiny hours of spring,
  Heads to my green-colored hills and
hosts of buildings on this side stretch in no billows high;
  Looking out on this scene of such joyful existence
now, I will stop questioning the condition of "happiness."

Part Two

TANKA

MIZUHO ŌTA
(1876–1955)

太田水穂

A priest all alone
taking a nap at midday—
beyond the eaves
of the abbot's chamber
the deep blueness of the sky.

*

As it becomes stormlike
in daytime, in the river bed
on the rocks there are
restless and confused
crows that are crying out.

YAICHI AIZU
(1881–1956)

会津八一

I stand as though
only I am existing
in heaven and earth—
at this solitariness,
Kannon,* you are smiling.

*

Coming stealthily,
who is it hitting the temple bell?
It is late at night
and t me for even the Buddha
to go into dreaming.

*

In the Lord Buddha's
drowsy eyes
the ancient
country fields of Yamato
Have their hazy existence.

* Image of Kannon (goddess of mercy), Nara

MOKICHI SAITŌ
(1882–1953)

斎藤茂吉

You water sp:der
against the streaming current
skating upstream—
your vigorousness, oh,
although it is a faint thing.

*

The faintly glowing
color of the maples,
when it fades away
before the falling of snow,
serenity in mountains.

*

This living creature,
each breath that I am taking,
is being observed
by one climbing up a window,
a praying mantis, alone.

Awakened
from winter sleep a frog
climbs up onto
the top of leftover snow
and stretches himself out flat.

*

The red-throated
chimney swallows, two of them,
upon the rafters—
and underneath, my mother
who is going to die now.

*

Those wild geese
do not pass over any more
within the sky
without limitat·on
the scattered snow is falling.

*

Very close to death
the mother I watch beside—
hush-hush—sounds
from far rice ponds, frogs crying
to heaven are being heard.

The clouds of springtime
come together at one side
around midday
by the far-off water reeds
the wild geese have settled down.

*

Being awakened
I was imagining that
the wild grasses
might be dropping down their seeds
at about this time of night.

*

The hush-hush
inside the falling of snow—
standing motionless,
a horse, his eyes.
Now he has blinked!

*

Crawling on the grass,
you firefly of the morning,
transient must be
this existence of mine.
Do not let me die, ever.

Mokichi Saitō * 145

Into spring mountains
I have come and am staying
one person alone
trying to hear the sound o
leaves fallen, dried, bent over.

*

(Mourning for Akutagawa)

Coming to a wall,
a lacewing May fly
is clinging to it—
the sheer transparency
of the wings, their mournfulness.

KENKICHI NAKAMURA

(1889–1934)

中村憲吉

Under the plane trees
young women are passing by,
upon their eyelids
is a color tinged with blood.
Summer has surely arrived.

*

My eye, watching,
I too become desolate
toward nightfall
from the harvested rice field
seeing stray grains being gathered.

*

On a mountain top
in springtime coldness
priests keep going back and forth
in black robes that are bulging
and mufflers that are white.

BUMMEI TSUCHIYA
(b. 1890)

土屋文明

With a happiness continuing all my life,
the day I began junior high school
The shoe shop of that time
is still here.
I come to a sudden standstill.

*

The past three mornings,
morning after morning
self-ornamenting,
the water-lily flower—
this morning it has not opened.

MIKIKO NAKAGAWA
(b. 1897)

中
河
幹
子

When that beam of light
came passing over the sea.
I as a whiteness
was revealed in the dark, and then
I saw I was all alone.

*

In the darkened fields
the very faintly burning
lights of the houses—
ah, they are more frail even
than the glowing of fireflies.

*

How far
will that wild duck still go
through evening waves
swollen in the open sea
where it struggles on alone?

FUMI SAITŌ
(b. 1909)

斎
藤

史

The pa'm of the hand
is not aware of dying as
without compulsion
it becomes cold and hardened
and only slightly shrunken.

*

The beating heart of myself
within the grease of myself
seems to be burning.
And what can be the reason
it is so cruelly thus?

*

In my inner self
where it stands up piercing me
the hollow cavern
has in times without a wind
the ultimate of darkness.

Ever more and more profound
will be the doubt in my mind
with which I must live
for the white robe of a god
was seen after it was stained.

*

With wings that will not ever
be folded a butterfly
will be made to soar
indefinitely in the white
hours of continuation.

*

Look at Orion
in loosened abandonment
to be for a night
become gentle as the spring
and balanced internally.

*

Within the blackened sea
of water where I now bathe
each time that I sink
I am being followed by
a solitary drowned man.

"Do not resemble me,
do not," I tell one I paint
in a picture as
a woman who is beautiful
with an adulteress's smile.

*

Both water and the earth
are frozen, no sound is made
in the cold night,
inside just myself
there is a lonely thing that does not freeze.

*

Dividing the wheat,
the place where construction is p'anned
has stakes pounded in—
like into thick animal skin
a needle being driven.

*

Because a tunnel
has a way for coming out,
with what is simp'y
a being happy there emerge
both bus and white butterfly.

As a landscape in the far distance
is how human life appears
and in autumn wind
upon the extended fields
a black locomotive goes.

TAEKO TAKAORI
(b. 1912)

高折妙子

Under thin rainfall
while descending a river
in a boa where
am all alone my shoulder
is slightly touched by willows.

*

A magpie bird,
singing, is pointed out to me—
moving the umbrella—
the boat being turned with
the oar—there, just ahead!

*

Cast upon the ground
the shadow of my own self
is being walked through
while my back is carrying
the brightness of the moon.

On he dawn-reddened
sky they are spreading out,
the singing cranes,
a thousand of the cranes,
and each voice a distinct voice.

*

Because the songbird
pauses while flying there is
a ceaseless swaying
of the willow's sheer branches
and a fall of loosened snow.

*

As on this day
after I die also
there will come again
from young persimmon leaves
a tapping sound of rain.

*

Now at evening
light accumulates around
a standing crane
and it is only there shining
continues without darkening.

Taeko Takaori * 1 5 5

The river's breadth
is narrowed by abundant
water hyacinths
too late for flowering but
green and profoundly quiet.

KUNIYO TAKAYASU
(b. 1913)

高安国世

Upon the water
time just does not exist
as something realized—
of the children, two of them,
we are father and mother!

＊

The same as a burning
is the air inside which
I am doing my work.
In the red pencil
the core has softened.

Part Three
HAIKU

Part Three

HAIKU

Poems of Autumn

HEKIGODŌ KAWAHIGASHI
(1873–1937)

河東碧梧桐

The first part o˙ spring—
wading in the water, there,
a single heron.

Flashes of lightning
in the ntervals between
the fireworks—now!

KYOSHI TAKAHAMA
(1874–1959)

高浜
虚子

A white peony
it is called—but even so,
a faint redness.

An autumn sky, and
under it wild camomile flowers
with some petals gone.

Over a ruined temple
where I had hoped to live
the moon is seen now.

One paulownia leaf
full of the rays of the sun
has fallen down.

On distant mountains
the shining of the sun—
Oh, withered fields!

Into the vast sky
stretching up at a slant,
winter trees.

With the pine-tree wind
go scooting and bustling about,
water spiders.

Flowing on by,
the leaves of radishes.
What swiftness!

A butterfly's
noises while eating something—
such quietness.

A dewy tree trunk.
Without a sound a locust
walking along.

Kyoshi Takahama * 163

The twilight darkness,
even in the floating duckweed,
how deep it is.

SEISENSUI OGIWARA
(b. 1884)

荻
原
井
泉
水

Your load being taken off,
what coldness, horse!
It is raining.

Drawing upon the ground,
the children play. Over them
sunlight of winter still lingers.

To where my own
teacups belong
in the house, returned.

With the moon being high
fishing boat lights
have each one singly settled into a place.

The dead volcano's
chilly surface—and also
wild strawberries.

Having a fatal disease,
how beautiful my fingernails
over the coals of charcoal!

SHŪŌSHI MIZUHARA
(b. 1892)

水原秋桜子

On the white birches
the moonlight is shining but
the pasture fence is in fog.

Stars above mountains—
this silkworm-raising village,
quiet and asleep.

My existence
facing chrysanthemums
becomes a silence.

Winter chrysanthemum—
what it wears is
only the glow of itself.

SUJŪ TAKANO
(b. 1893)

高
野
素
十

The girl cutting reeds
turns her face toward the sky
and combs out her hair.

A temple room's
big heavy eaves—out comes
a spring butterfly.

Now someone else
is beginning to cut down
the distant reeds.

A spider's web—
one strand of it goes across
the front of a lily.

TAKAKO HASHIMOTO
(1899–1963)

All plucked off—
a chicken's feathers lying
under a winter moon.

Into a white peach
the edge of a blade is thrust—
the seed has been cut.

SANKI SAITŌ
(1900–1962)

西東三鬼

Without an ending,
the falling snow.
What will it bring?

A tumbled-down
scarecrow's face
and over it the sky.

SEISHI YAMAGUCHI
(b. 1901)

山口誓子

While enduring
the loneliness of learning,
replenishing the charcoal.

Up to the summer weeds
wheels of a steam engine
come and stop.

Under a winter moon,
with shallow water,
a river flows.

The string of a kite
invisible upon the sky
visible on a finger.

The race-starting pistol
sounds upon the hard-looking surface
of the swimming pool.

KUSATAO NAKAMURA
(b. 1901)

中村草田男

Sailing in autumn,
being inside
one huge and deep blue disk.

In the baby carriage,
onto the joggled apple
continuing to hold.

Falling snow!
The Meiji period, far
away it has gone.

Greenness everywhere
and inside it my own child's
teeth starting to grow out.

石
田
波
鄉

The captive eagle
because of loneliness is
flapping his wings—oh!

Waiting for the bus,
springtime on the avenue
cannot be doubted.

KIYOKO TSUDA
(b. 1920)

What a burdensome
life for the grasshoppers to
experience frost.

To be a mistress
is enough to tame me and
I cut a watermelon.

SHIGENOBU TAKAYANAGI
(b. 1923)

高柳重信

A rainbow's body bent backward
at its summit
         a hanging gallows.

Ashes are falling
In a tavern on a hill
firewood burns up its body.

Where sea
waves surge forward at
a river's mouth
sickness is
in a young bat lying there.

Growing old
and lunatic

in a swamp
a serpent
blossoms with a red flower.

They resemble stakes
gravestones
standing there in rows
as though hammered in.

Hear a war drum sound
and desolately
on autumn
become a bruisemark.

BIOGRAPHICAL NOTES

TAKAMURA, KŌTARŌ (1883–1956). He was the son of a noted sculptor. At first he wrote only in the tanka form, but, after leaving Japan in 1906 to study sculpture in the United States, he read Whitman's poetry and started writing free verse. His four years abroad included much time in France, where he read such poets as Verlaine, Baudelaire, and Rimbaud and was influenced by Rodin. Back in Japan he was known as a strong humanist. The interest in socialism which he had for a while is apparent in some of his poems, such as *Another Rotating Thing*. When his wife Chieko died after seven years of insanity he wrote a book of poems about her which became his most popular work. However, he is also highly respected for some half-dozen other volumes of poetry as well as for his lifelong activity as a sculptor.

HAGIWARA, SAKUTARŌ (1886–1942). He began to write tanka when a junior high school student and continued writing in this form for about ten years. By 1914 he had begun to write free verse and by 1917 his first book of poems had been published. This work, which was titled *Howling at the Moon*, has been called the most epoch-making volume in the history of Japanese poetry. In it, he used colloquial language to express himself as a modern, with a genius which gave greatness to his work. His *Blue Cat* of 1923 furthered the developments of his first book. His work includes several other volumes of poetry as well as essays and criticism. Three separate editions of his complete works have been published in Japan.

MURŌ, SAISEI (1889–1962). After finishing primary school he became an office boy in a rural law court; his interest in literature started at this time. He began by writing haiku, but in 1918 he published two volumes of free verse, *Poems of Love* and *Little Lyric Pieces*. With Hagiwara he also issued the magazine *Sentiment*. It was through his acquaintance with the great short-story writer Akutagawa that he started writing fiction and established himself as a novelist. At the same time he published many books of essentially lyrical poetry.

OZAKI, KIHACHI (1892–   ). After graduating from a commercial high school in Tokyo he studied French and German. He was a friend of Takamura. The poetry of his more than ten volumes reflects his lyrical attitude toward nature. He himself lived in the highlands and fields. He has done considerable translation work also, including writings of Romain Rolland and Herman Hesse.

KANEKO, MITSUHARU (1895–   ). By the time he was twenty-four he had tried two universities and an art academy and published a book of poetry. Soon afterward he went to Europe for two and a half years. There he lived mostly in Belgium and read the work of Verhaeren and Baudelaire. He returned to Japan, but in 1929 left again for seven years in the Near East, France, and Belgium. While abroad he did all kinds of menial labor to support himself. In his poetry there is strong criticism and satire against the conventionalities of Japan. One of his seventeen poetry books, *The Tragedy of Man*, won the Yomiuri Literary Award in 1953.

TSUBOI, SHIGEJI (1898–   ). Shodo Island in the Inland Sea was his birthplace. When halfway through Waseda University in

Tokyo he quit, but at the age of twenty-five he was issuing the avant-garde magazine *Red and Black* and taking part in the socialist movement. Twice he was imprisoned in Japan during the difficult years. After the war he was one of the founders of the New Japan Literary Society. About ten of his books have been published.

SASAZAWA, YOSHIAKI (1898–   ). He was a graduate of the Tokyo University of Foreign Studies. While still young he was especially interested in the poetry of Heine. The magazine *Poetry and Poetics* counted him as an active group-member and, with Shirō Murano and others, he issued the maga zine*Neue Sachlichkeit*. He developed an interest in Rilke's work and he has written several books about him. Some ten volumes of his poetry have been published.

KURAHARA, SHINJIRŌ (1889–1965). The southern Japanese island of Kyushu was his early home. While in high school he started reading such classical Chinese poets as Li Po and Tu Fu. After coming to Tokyo at the age of nineteen he studied ceramics for a year, but eventually he graduated from the French literature department of Keio University. The publication of Hagiwara's *Blue Cat* strongly affected him. His interest in Buddhist philosophy appears in several of his poems, such as *Fox*. *Footprints* was his last poem, composed in bed just three weeks before his death and written down by one of his friends. The last of his six volumes of poetry won the Yomiuri Literary Award in 1965.

MIYOSHI, TATSUJI (1900–1964). After attending the Military Academy for a while, training to become an officer, he eventually took a degree in French literature from Tokyo University. In his boyhood he had written haiku, but his first book, *Survey Ship*, 1930, was of modern verse. This was followed by other poetry books by which he established a new lyricism in Japan. His work also includes criticism, essays, and translations of such writers as Zola, Baudelaire, Jammes, and Gide.

KITAGAWA, FUYUHIKO (1900–   ). His childhood was spent in Manchuria. He began poetry writing while still in junior high school and his first book was published in 1925. In 1928 he was associated with the magazine *Poetry and Poetics*. He was also associated with the new prose-poem movement. Since 1950 he has issued the poetry magazine *Time*. He is known for his stand on neo-realism. The metaphors by which he expresses his socialistic consciousness are characteristic of his poetry.

MURANO, SHIRŌ (1901–   ). As did many other Japanese poets, he began writing haiku when just a junior high school student, and he wrote free-haiku under Seisensui Ogiwara. After entering Keio University he became interested in German poetry and the work of Hagiwara also influenced him. His first book came out in 1926. Of the approximately ten books of poetry he has published, *Gymnastics* and *A Strayed Sheep* are considered especially noteworthy. The latter received the Yomiuri Literary Award in 1960. He is one of the leading critics of poetry.

TAKAHASHI, SHINKICHI (1901–   ). After leaving a commercial high school on Shikoku Island he came to Tokyo and led a vagabond life. The book he published in 1923, *Poems of Dadaist Shinkichi*, gained attention for him in the literary world of Tokyo. In his twenties he lived in a temple and read Buddhist literature. Gradually his poetry came to express Zen in a surrealist style. He also writes fiction and essays.

TAKENAKA, IKU (1904–   ). He was born in Kobe. While a university student he began publishing his poems in several magazines. From the ages of twenty-four to twenty-six he traveled in

Europe with an artist friend. In the meantime he was taking part in the magazine *Poetry and Poetics*. In 1947 he founded a noted poetry magazine for children, *Giraffe*. He has published about seven books of poetry.

ITŌ, SEI (1905–1969). The northern island of Hokkaido was his birthplace. While still in a commercial high school there, he came to be influenced by Yeats as well as by Hagiwara. When only twenty he published his first book of poetry. From 1928 on, he was active in Tokyo. His second book of poetry appeared in 1937, but later he turned to other kinds of writing and became an important novelist and critic. He is also known for translations of D. H. Lawrence and James Joyce. His complete works have already been published in fourteen volumes.

ITŌ, SHIZUO (1906–1953). While attending Kyoto University he wrote tanka and keenly felt the influence of Hölderlin and Rilke. After graduation he became a teacher in Osaka, where he remained. His first book, *Sad Songs for My Dearest*, brought him fame when it was greatly admired by Hagiwara. Only three more volumes appeared before his early death, and there was a posthumous *Collected Poems*.

TAKAMI, JUN (1907–1965). While in high school he edited a little magazine and had several Dadaist poems published. When twentyone he formed a league of leftist artists with Tsuboi and others. In 1933 he was arrested for his activities, but later his outlook changed. He graduated from Tokyo University with a degree in English, became a writer of fiction, and during the war was a government reporter in Southeast Asia. Afterward he started writing poetry again while recovering from tuberculosis. Just before his death from cancer he published the poetry book *From the Abyss of Death*, which impressed many people. His complete works have been issued in six volumes.

AIDA, TSUNAO (1914–   ). Tokyo was his birthplace. In 1940 he served in Nanking as a volunteer in Military Intelligence. There he knew the poet Shimpei Kusano and other writers who became noted after the war. In 1957 he published the poetry book *Salt-lake*, which was awarded the Kōtarō Takamura Prize. He is employed by a Tokyo publisher.

YOSHIOKA, MINORU (1919–   ). During his boyhood in Tokyo he began writing tanka and haiku. For a while he worked for a publisher, but in 1941 he was drafted and sent to Manchuria. His first book of poetry came out just two days after Pearl Harbor. His third book, *Priest*, published in 1958, won an award. He works for the same publisher as Aida.

KURODA, SABURŌ (1919–   ). During the war he was in Java. After returning to Japan he became a member of the Waste Land group. About half a dozen books of his poetry have been published. He now edits the monthly magazine *Poetry and Criticism* and works for the Japan Broadcasting Association.

ANZAI, HITOSHI (1919–   ). Around 1940, when he was associated with several writers on his home island of Kyushu, he began to write poetry. Soon after, he became a reporter on the Asahi Newspaper and continued this work for fifteen years. Then he worked for the Japan Design Center. His first book of poetry, which was published in 1955, has been followed by several more volumes.

NAKAGIRI, MASAO (1919–   ). He lived in Kobe until he was twenty and there edited two little magazines of poetry which were part of the Waste Land movement. At present he works for the Yomiuri Newspaper in Tokyo. He has written essays on contemporary English and American poets as well as composing his own poetry.

AYUKAWA, NOBUO (1920–   ). After 1937 he was associated with several poetry magazines. When twenty-two he left the English department of Waseda University, Tokyo, and was drafted into the army. Two years later he was returned to Japan from Sumatra as a disabled soldier and he became one of those active in the Waste Land movement. His collected poems appeared in 1955, and he also wrote a number of volumes of essays and translated some of T. S. Eliot's essays.

TAMURA, RYŪICHI (1923–   ). When in his teens he began writing poetry. He graduated from Meiji University, Tokyo, and edited the monthly magazine *Waste Land*. His first book, published when he was thirty-three, was *Four Thousand Days and Nights*. In 1962 his second book of poetry, *World Without Words*, was given the Kōtarō Takamura Prize. So far he has published about four books of poetry and translated a number of books, including some by T. S. Eliot.

YAMAMOTO, TARŌ (1925–   ). He is a graduate of the German literature department of Tokyo University. One of his four books of poetry received a Kōtarō Takamura Prize. In Tokyo he is a university teacher.

TANIKAWA, SHUNTARŌ (1931–   ). When he was twenty-one his first book of poetry, *The Solitude of Two Billion Light Years*, was praised by Miyoshi. In addition to half a dozen books of poetry he has written dramas and essays.

ŌOKA, MAKOTO (1931–   ). He is a graduate of Tokyo University's department of Japanese literature. Four volumes of his poetry have been published. As a critic of literature and the arts, he has also published many books on these subjects in addition to translations of books on art.

SAWAI, ATSUHIRO (1940–   ). While in the English literature department of Kyoto University he wrote tanka and some of
them were published in magazines. His first book of poetry came
out in 1967 and was well received by several Tokyo critics. He
is now teaching English in Kyoto.

TANKA POETS

ŌTA, MIZUHO (1876–1955). He was strongly against the realism
of Mokichi Saitō, and himself advocated an Oriental symbolism
based on Bashō's haiku and on the tanka of the 12th-century *Shin
Kokinshū*. His complete works have been published in ten volumes.

AIZU, YAICHI (1881–1956). The classical history of the ancient
Nara period strongly interested him. He was quite rare for a tanka
poet in that he never belonged to any poetic group. As a professor
at Waseda University, Tokyo, he taught the history of Chinese art
and of Nara, as well as English literature. His complete works are
in nine volumes.

SAITŌ, MOKICHI (1882–1953). His first book of tanka, published in 1913, was very highly acclaimed and began a revival of
interest in the *Manyōshū*. After studying medicine in Tokyo and
doing research in psychiatry in Vienna and Munich, he operated
his own hospital in Tokyo. His complete works in fifty-six volumes
include seventeen tanka books as well as essays and criticism.

NAKAMURA, KENKICHI (1889–1934). He was closely acquainted with Mokichi Saitō and a member of the group associated
with his magazine *Yew Tree*. His complete works in four volumes
include tanka, essays, criticism, and research on Shiki Masaoka
and the 8th-century poet Akahito Yamabe.

TSUCHIYA, BUMMEI (1890–   ). He also was a friend of Mokichi Saitō, and one of the chief associates of the magazine *Yew Tree*. After the founder's death he was responsible for the magazine's development. At first romantic and lyrical, his tanka later gradually became realistic. He did many books of research on the *Manyōshū*.

NAKAGAWA, MIKIKO (1897–   ). The island of Shikoku was her birthplace but Tokyo has been her home for many years. Since the last war she has edited the tanka magazine *Columbine*. In addition to poetry, several volumes of her essays have been published. She is a professor at Kyōritsu Women's College.

SAITŌ, FUMI (1909–   ). She began writing in her late teens, influenced by her father's poetry. (He was an army general who wrote tanka.) During the war she moved to the mountain area of Nagano, where she has made her home ever since. She is one of the most noted of contemporary tanka poets and her imaginative imagery is unique. In addition to half a dozen volumes of poetry she has published several books of essays.

TAKAORI, TAEKO (1912–   ). Her father was the noted artist Kansetsu Hashimoto and her home has always been in Kyoto. After graduating from the Sacred Heart Women's Academy in Tokyo she traveled through Europe and spent a year in England. She has been abroad many times since. She is leader of several tanka groups in the Kyoto-Osaka area and has published three volumes of her tanka.

TAKAYASU, KUNIYO (1913–   ). He was born in Osaka and graduated from Kyoto University's German literature department. Under Bummei Tsuchiya he studied tanka and in 1954 he began issuing the magazine *Tower*. In 1957 he studied at the University of Munich, with a special interest in German lyric poets, and he has translated Rilke, Goethe, and Heine. He is a professor at Kyoto University and has published seven volumes of tanka.

HAIKU POETS

KAWAHIGASHI, HEKIGODŌ (1873–1937). He attended junior and senior high school with Kyoshi Takahama and they were both influenced by their master, Shiki Masaoka. But later these two came to have different ideas. Kawahigashi's haiku became more realistic, freer, and less literary, but increasingly difficult to understand.

TAKAHAMA, KYOSHI (1874–1959). He too was greatly influenced by his master, Shiki Masaoka. As a close friend of the great novelist Sōseki Natsume, he wrote fiction for a while. The careers of many contemporary haiku poets developed from his magazine *Cuckoo*. His complete works are in twelve volumes.

OGIWARA, SEISENSUI (1884–   ). Although he was once a disciple of Kawahigashi and helped issue his magazine, he evolved different ideas and traveled all over Japan on behalf of his own haiku movement. He also published many books on Bashō and Issa. At present he is known as the leader in free-haiku.

IIDA, DAKOTSU (1885–1962). After entering Waseda University in Tokyo he started writing haiku under Kyoshi Takahama. Although many new movements occurred in haiku, he never changed his style. And, after returning to his country home, he continued to write poetry describing the rural area where he remained until his death.

MIZUHARA, SHŪŌSHI (1892–   ). He was a doctor in the Ministry of the Imperial Household and ran a hospital. He began by writing tanka, but later switched to haiku. When he became dissatisfied with the haiku attitude of his teacher Takahama, he published his own magazine, *Ashibi*, and from it several excellent poets developed. His haiku movement is based on modern intellectuality and a tanka-like lyricism.

TAKANO, SUJŪ (1893–   ). As a Tokyo University medical student he became acquainted with Shūōshi Mizuhara and started writing haiku. He became a professor of medicine but continued to work at haiku under Kyoshi Takahama, as one of those most close to him and his attitudes.

HASHIMOTO, TAKAKO (1899–1963). After her marriage she went from Tokyo to the southern island of Kyushu for a while, and there she became interested in haiku. She studied under Kyoshi Takahama and then later under Seishi Yamaguchi. In Nara after the war she organized the Nara Haiku Association with Sanki Saitō and others. Five books of her haiku have been published.

SAITŌ, SANKI (1900–1962). From 1925 to 1929 he had a dental office in Singapore. After returning to Japan he became interested in haiku through a haiku club of the patients at the hospital where he worked. He was a permanent member of the group associated with Seishi Yamaguchi's magazine *Sirius* and followed them in rejecting conventional lyricism. He was also chief editor of the magazine *Haiku*.

YAMAGUCHI, SEISHI (1901–   ). Although born in Kyoto he spent part of his childhood in Sakhalin. In Tokyo later, with Shūōshi Mizuhara, he studied haiku under Kyoshi Masaoka. When he became dissatisfied with conservatism in haiku, he issued his own magazine, *Sirius*. His haiku subjects were sought in the modern city and lyricism was excluded.

NAKAMURA, KUSATAO (1901–   ). He was born in the Japanese consulate at Amoy, China, and brought to Japan when he was four. As a Tokyo University student, he read Mokichi Saitō and became interested in both tanka and haiku poetry. Although he studied under Shūōshi Mizuhara, his use of allegorical or metaphorical expressions often made his haiku difficult to understand. He is, however, noted as a humanistic haiku poet. He is a professor at Seikei University, Tokyo.

ISHIDA, HAKYŌ (1913–1969). He also studied haiku under Shūōshi Mizuhara and was an important member of the *Ashibi* magazine group. As others did, he became independent and began his own magazine. A lung disease contracted in China after he was drafted into the army weakened his health. His later haiku turned from concern with lyricism to a humanistic attitude, and in 1954 he was awarded the Yomiuri Literary Prize.

TSUDA, KIYOKO (1920–   ). The ancient capital of Nara was her birthplace. She graduated from the Normal School there and, after the war, started studying haiku under Takako Hashimoto and Seishi Yamaguchi. She is now teaching at an Osaka school.

TAKAYANAGI, SHIGENOBU (1923–   ). He was born in Tokyo and graduated from the law department of Waseda University. In 1936 he started to publish his haiku in magazines and since then he has edited several haiku magazines. He also writes critical essays on haiku. About half a dozen books of his haiku have been published.

SELECTED BIBLIOGRAPHY

Blyth, R. H.: *Haiku,* 4 vols., Hokuseidō, Tokyo, 1952.

―――: *Japanese Humour,* Japan Tourist Bureau, Tokyo, 1957.

―――: *Senryū: Japanese Satirical Verses,* Hokuseidō, Tokyo, 1949.

Borton, Hugh, et al.: *A Selected List of Books and Articles on Japan in English, French and German,* Harvard University Press, Cambridge, 1954.

Bownas, Geoffrey, and Thwaite, Anthony: *The Penguin Book of Japanese Verse,* Penguin Books, Harmondsworth, 1964.

Brower, Robert H., and Miner, Earl: *Japanese Court Poetry,* Stanford University Press, Stanford, 1961.

―――, trans.: *Fujiwara Teika's "Superior Poems of Our Time,"* Stanford University Press, Stanford, 1961.

Corman, Cid, and Kamaike, Susumu, trans.: *Kusano Shimpei,* Iwasaki Arts Co., Tokyo, 1966.

―――: *Back Roads to Far Towns: Bashō's "Oku-no-hosomichi,"* Grossman, New York, 1968.

Fukuda, Rikutarō, and Konō, Ichirō: *An Anthology of Modern Japanese Poetry,* Kenkyusha, Tokyo, 1957.

Henderson, Harold G.: *The Bamboo Broom,* Houghton Mifflin, Boston, 1934.

―――: *An Introduction to Haiku,* Doubleday Anchor Books, New York, 1958.

―――: *Haiku in English,* Charles E. Tuttle Co., Tokyo and Rutland, Vermont, 1965.

Japanese Literature in European Languages, A Bibliography, Japan P.E.N. Club, Tokyo, 1961.

Keene, Donald: *Anthology of Japanese Literature*, Grove Press, New York, 1955.

————: *Japanese Literature*, Grove Press, New York, 1955.

————: *Modern Japanese Literature*, Grove Press, New York, 1956.

Kitasono, Katsue: "Eight Contemporary Japanese Poets," *New World Writing*, New York, vol. 6, Oct. 1954.

Miner, Earl, trans.: *Japanese Poetic Diaries*, Stanford University Press, Stanford, 1969.

Miyamori, Asatarō: *An Anthology of Haiku, Ancient and Modern*, Maruzen, Tokyo, 1932; reprinted by Taiseidō, Tokyo, 1956.

————: *An Anthology of Japanese Poems*, Maruzen, Tokyo, 1938.

————: *Masterpieces of Japanese Poetry*, Maruzen, Tokyo, 1936.

Ninomiya, Takamichi, and Enright, D. J.: *The Poetry of Living Japan*, Grove Press, New York, 1957.

Sakanishi, Shio, trans.: *A Handful of Sand*, Marshall Jones, Boston, 1934. Tanka of Takuboku Ishikawa.

————: *Songs of a Cowherd*, Marshall Jones, Boston, 1936. Tanka of Sachio Itō.

————: *Tangled Hair*, Marshall Jones, Boston, 1935. Tanka of Akiko Yosano.

————: "The Women Writers of Today," *Japan Quarterly*, Tokyo, vol. 2, Oct./Dec. 1955, pp. 489–95.

Satō, Satoru, and Urdang, Constance: "Contemporary Poetry in Japan," *Poetry*, Chicago, May 1956, vol. 88, no. 2. Modern Japanese poetry number.

————: "What Is Good Translation of Poetry?" *The East-West Review*, Kyoto, vol. 2, no. 3, spring–summer 1966. Asian poetry number.

Stewart, Harold: *A Net of Fireflies, Japanese Haiku and Haiku Paintings*, Charles E. Tuttle Co., Tokyo and Rutland, Vermont, 1960.

Ueda, Makoto: "Japanese Literature Since World War II," *The Literary Review*, Teaneck, New Jersey, vol. 6, no. 1, autumn 1962. Japan number.

————: *Zeami, Bashō, Yeats, Pound: A Study in Japanese and English Poetics*, Mouton & Co., The Hague, 1965.

————: *Literary and Art Theories in Japan*, Western Reserve University Press, Cleveland, 1967.

————: "Translations of Eighteen Poems," *The East-West Review*, Kyoto, vol. 2, no. 3, spring–summer 1966. Asian poetry number.

Uyehara, Yukuo, and Sinclair, Marjorie, trans.: *A Grass Path, The Poems of Kotomichi Okuma*, University of Hawaii Press, Honolulu, 1955.

Wilson, Graeme, trans.: *Face at the Bottom of the World*, Charles E. Tuttle Co., Tokyo and Rutland, Vermont, 1969. Poems of Sakutarō Hagiwara.

Yamagiwa, Joseph K.: *Japanese Literature of the Shōwa Period*, University of Michigan Press, Ann Arbor, 1959.

Yasuda, Kenneth: *The Japanese Haiku: Its Essential Nature, History, and Possibilities in English, with Selected Examples*, Charles E. Tuttle Co., Tokyo and Rutland, Vermont, 1957.

————: trans.: *A Pepper Pod*, Knopf, New York, 1947.

————: trans., *Land of the Reed Plains, Ancient Japanese Lyrics from the Manyōshū*, Charles E. Tuttle Co., Tokyo and Rutland, Vermont, 1960.

————: trans., *Minase Sangin Hyakuin, A Poem of One Hundred Lines Composed by Three Poets at Minase*, Kōgakusha, Tokyo, 1956.

————: trans., *Myriad Leaves*, Hosokawa, Tokyo, 1949. The Manyōshū.

Yuasa, Nobuyuki, trans.: *Bashō: The Narrow Road to the Deep North and Other Travel Sketches*, Penguin Books, Harmondsworth, 1966.

————: *The Year of My Life: A Translation of Issa's "Oragaharu,"* University of California Press, Berkeley, 1960.

INDEX OF POETS